# The Man Behind the Magic

W9-AJB-502

WITHDRAWN

Photo credit: Rush Johnson

# The Man Behind the Magic

## THE STORY OF WALT DISNEY

By Katherine and Richard Greene

VIKING

*This book is dedicated to our parents*
*and to our children, Benjamin and Sandra*

VIKING
Published by the Penguin Group
Penguin Putnam Books for Young Readers, 345 Hudson Street, New York, New York,
10014, U.S.A.
Penguin Books Ltd, 27 Wrights Lane, London W8 5TZ, England
Penguin Books Australia Ltd, Ringwood, Victoria, Australia
Penguin Books Canada Ltd, 10 Alcorn Avenue, Toronto, Ontario, Canada M4V 3B2
Penguin Books (N.Z.) Ltd, 182–190 Wairau Road, Auckland 10, New Zealand

Penguin Books Ltd, Registered Offices: Harmondsworth, Middlesex, England

First published in 1991 by Viking Penguin, a division of Penguin Books USA Inc.
This edition with a new chapter and foreword published in 1998 by Viking,
a member of Penguin Putnam Books for Young Readers.

1  3  5  7  9  10  8  6  4  2

Copyright © Richard and Katherine Greene, 1991, 1998
Foreword copyright © Diane Disney Miller, 1998
All rights reserved

Still from OSWALD THE LUCKY RABBIT copyright © 1998 by Universal Studios Publishing
Rights. All Rights Reserved.

Academy Awards® photograph copyright of the Academy of Motion Picture Arts and Sciences.

The Library of Congress has catalogued the hardcover edition as follows:

Greene, Katherine.
The man behind the magic : the story of Walt Disney / by Katherine
and Richard Greene.
p.  cm.
Summary: Follows the life of Walt Disney from his boyhood on a
Missouri farm through his struggles as a young animator to his
building of a motion picture and amusement park empire.
ISBN 0-670-82259-0
1. Disney, Walt 1901–1966—Juvenile literature.   2. Animators—
United States—Biography—Juvenile literature.   [1. Disney, Walt,
1901–1966.   2. Motion pictures—Biography.]   I. Greene,  Richard
(Richard Harris)   II. Title.
NC1766.U52D5315 1990
791.43'092—dc20   [B]   [92]      90-32936     CIP     AC

This edition ISBN 0-670-88476-6

Printed in U.S.A.
Set in Electra

This book makes reference to various Disney copyrighted characters, trademarks, marks and
registered marks owned by The Walt Disney Company and Disney Enterprises, Inc.

# Contents

Color Photographs Follow Page 112

# Foreword

I love to read. I always have. It began with the Winnie-the-Pooh stories when I was very young. Then Mary Poppins, dog and horse stories, Nancy Drew, Charles Dickens, the Brontë sisters, and so forth. Now I read just about anything I can get my hands on that holds my interest. But I especially enjoy biography.

When reading a biography, however, I often wonder if the author is treating the subject fairly and honestly. When dealing with a person long dead, even the most earnest biography must rely on previously published accounts. In the best of all worlds, all biographies would be scrupulously honest with their subjects. Unfortunately, that is not always so.

I met Katherine and Richard Greene in 1986. They had been to Disney World, thoroughly enjoyed it, and wanted to buy a book about the man who had created it for their fourteen-year-old nephew. They were disappointed to find that nothing suitable existed that would be appealing to someone of that age and they became determined to do something about it.

The Greenes were not content merely to gather information from previous publications or accept others' opinions of Walt Disney. They embarked on a five-year-long odyssey of discovery, visiting the sites of my father's life and meeting and interviewing childhood friends, family, co-workers, and others who knew him well. They formed opinions of their own, not pre-conceived, but fresh ones.

And I learned more about my father and his family through their process,

The Greenes never forgot their target reader, and their biography of my father is eminently readable, with appeal not only to a young reader but to adults who are unwilling to deal with the plethora of dry dates, facts, and names most biographies insist on including. My aunt Ruth Disney Beecher praised their work because she felt that the Greenes dealt honestly with her family's life.

My father used to say, "Why would anyone want to do a biography of me? I'm a pretty dull character—there's no scandal in my life." But Dad's life was anything but dull, and he loved to talk about it.

My sister and I—and others—heard the same stories many times over. He loved to recount tales of childhood adventures in Marceline, Missouri, of his career beginnings in Kansas City, and of his experiences in France as an ambulance driver at the end of World War I.

Unfortunately, some writers have sought to embellish the life of this "pretty dull," scandal-free guy with a lot of mean-spirited distortion and inaccuracies that neither my father nor any of us would have thought possible.

*The Man Behind the Magic: The Story of Walt Disney* is an honest and sincere effort by two experienced writers and researchers. Enjoy it. Trust it. I said when it first came out, "I am grateful for it."

My gratitude and appreciation for this book grows.

Diane Disney Miller
June 1998

# The Man Behind the Magic

# Mickey Is Born

© Walt Disney Enterprises

*"Walt never thought he was beaten at anything—ever."*
—LILLIAN DISNEY

It was a gloomy Thursday in March, 1928, and twenty-six-year-old Walt Disney and his wife Lilly were about to return home to California from New York City. Before boarding the train, Walt wrote a telegram to his brother, and business partner, Roy.

*Don't worry*, it read, *Everything OK. Will give details when arrive.*

Short and sweet. And also a lie. The truth was that the Disneys' cartoon studio was nearly ruined.

Oswald the Lucky Rabbit had been kidnapped.

A cartoon bunny with long, black, floppy ears and a rambunctious nature, Oswald had been Walt's ticket to success. After seven years of struggling in the competitive animation business, this creation of his had won over critics and moviegoers alike. Children wrote to the studio to ask for the rabbit's autograph. Stores carried Oswald candy bars, Oswald stencil sets, and Oswald buttons.

Walt had come to New York to ask for more money for his Oswald cartoons. He was sure that Charlie Mintz—the dapper, thin man with slicked-back hair who distributed Walt's cartoons to movie theaters—would not hesitate to

3

reward such great success. Mintz bolstered Walt's confidence when he invited the couple to eat with him at the posh Hotel Astor. The lunch was full of light chatter and praise—no discussion of money. "This is the talented guy I've been telling you about," Mintz told friends who dropped by their table. "You mark my words. This boy will go far."

Walt didn't get much farther than Mintz's Times Square office.

When the two men returned there for the real business at hand, Mintz turned stoney-faced. There would be no more money for Walt, he said. In fact, there would be less; so little that Walt wouldn't be able to stay in business. What was Walt supposed to do? Simple. He could give up his own business and come to work for Mintz.

Shocked, Walt threatened to take Oswald to another distributor. Mintz was unfazed. He revealed that he had been plotting for weeks to force Walt to become his employee. Even as Walt was celebrating Oswald's success, Mintz had secretly hired away all but one of Disney's animators with the lure of more money and secure jobs.

Walt couldn't believe that his artists would do this to him. His staff was largely made up of young men he had known since they were teenagers. Several of them had gotten their first jobs with him. He had trained them, encouraged them, entertained them in his home. As far as Walt was concerned, he was the captain and they were his loyal crew on a happy voyage to fame and fortune.

He raced back to the hotel where a telephone call to Roy confirmed Mintz's story. The brothers decided that they could find new artists if they needed to. It would be difficult, but not impossible. Still, they needed a new distributor. Walt stalled Mintz for several weeks while he tried to find one.

When Mintz got wind of Walt's efforts he gave him a second piece of alarming news: Although Walt had breathed life into Oswald, formed his personality, and overseen the development of his appearance, legally Oswald did not belong to the Disneys. The fine print in the contracts said that Oswald belonged to Universal Pictures. Mintz had complete control over the rabbit's future.

Unwilling to work for Mintz, Walt decided to walk away from Oswald. As for the animators, he warned Mintz: "These boys will do the same thing to you, Charlie. If they'll do it to me, they'll do it to you. Now, watch out for them."

4

That's exactly what came to pass. Only a few years later, the same animators left Mintz for greener pastures. Right now, however, it was Walt who was on the losing end. He and Roy were the proud owners of a cartoon studio with two artists (counting Walt) and no characters to animate.

As the conductor bellowed "All aboard," Walt took Lilly's hand and helped her clamber up the high steps onto the train. They walked to their private compartment and sat down without saying a word. Although Roy wouldn't hear the complete details of the Mintz disaster for a few more days, Walt could think of little else.

The tale of what followed has been told so many times that it is shrouded in the mist of legend; it's impossible now to know exactly where truth ends and Walt's love for a good story begins.

But the way Walt enjoyed telling it later, once he and Lilly had started their three-day trip back home, something wonderful happened.

He took out a big yellow pad, and as the train started to steam and lurch forward he doodled while Lilly relaxed.

As they chugged away from the densely packed East Coast out into the gentle hills of Pennsylvania and the flat green farmlands of Ohio and Indiana, the insistent vibration of the train settled Walt's jangled nerves and his doodlings began to take some shape.

Now he concentrated on circles, big circles and little ones, connecting and crossing to form first a body, then a head and ears. An elongated circle turned into a nose of sorts. Stick legs were added and the figure came close to completion.

Lilly watched the pencil sketches take on a life of their own and realized that it was a mouse Walt was drawing.

"What do you think of the name 'Mortimer Mouse'?" asked Walt, staring down at his work with the first smile he had smiled in a thousand miles.

"Mortimer? That's a funny name for a mouse," said Lilly, grinning along with Walt. "Yes, I'm not sure I like the name Mortimer very much at all. . . ."

The train rolled along and Walt doodled some more on the ears.

"How about Mickey?" asked Lilly.

In the months that followed, Oswald was forgotten, as Walt turned his attention to the promising rodent. After Mickey Mouse came Donald Duck, Goofy, and Pluto. The pioneering cartoon features of *Snow White, Pinocchio,* and

*Fantasia* were followed by movie classics like *Treasure Island, 20,000 Leagues Under the Sea,* and *Mary Poppins.* Disneyland and Walt Disney World created a brand-new concept in family entertainment.

"Everything Walt touched worked out well," Lilly remarked admiringly sixty years after the birth of Mickey. "He always was a lucky man."

No question about it. If guardian angels exist, Walt's worked overtime.

But there was another side to the story. At many points in his career—like the day he lost Oswald—Walt Disney had good reason to think of himself as the unluckiest guy around. The story of his life is one with a failure for every success and a disappointment for every victory. None of his accomplishments came cheaply, none ever satisfied him. He was endlessly driven by a ravenous hunger for new fields to conquer.

The most private of men in the most public of endeavors, Walt remained a mystery even to those people who worked most closely with him. He was called tyrant and saint, bully and benefactor. Though he acknowledged that many of his employees were better artists than he, they turned to Walt for inspiration. Musicians were astonished at his ability to lead them to their best work, though he could barely carry a tune. He had no formal architectural or engineering training, yet the most talented architects and engineers in the world were honored to work by his side.

Many tried to understand him, to explain him in a few well-chosen words or pithy anecdotes. But the very few who were close to Walt Disney knew that such efforts were doomed.

"You won't find anyone who can really explain the magic of Walt," said Disney artist Peter Ellenshaw. "People see him either in black or white, but he was an extraordinary mixture. He was a common man who was endowed with a touch of magic."

# First Love

© Walt Disney Enterprises

*"More things of importance happened to me in Marceline than have happened since—or are likely to in the future."*
—WALT DISNEY

*Walt at ten months*

The magic began in Marceline.

Walt was four years old when his father decided to buy a 45-acre farm on the outskirts of the tiny town, halfway between St. Louis and Kansas City, Missouri. A carpenter and builder, Elias Disney no longer wanted his five children exposed to the saloons and crime-filled streets of Chicago, where Walt was born on December 5, 1901. So, in the spring of 1906, the Disney family packed up their furniture, cooking gear, and the family Bible and moved to Missouri.

To Walt, the new farm was paradise.

Weeping-willow trees, cedars, and silver maples dotted the family's lush front yard. In back of the white frame house, apple orchards were rich with the scent of springtime blossoms.

In the fall, Walt saw his first harvest and the community teamwork of the farm. His brothers, Roy, 13, Raymond, 15, and Herbert, 17, labored shoulder-to-shoulder with their father. Neighbors pitched in on big chores. Together, they slaughtered hogs, one at a time, dipping the carcasses into boiling pots and scraping off the short prickly hairs. Farm wives spread tables of cornbread,

7

chicken, and pies under the weeping willows. Young children like Walt fetched water for the thirsty crew.

As he grew older, Walt's world expanded from the farm to the neighborhood and nearby town. "Sometimes, if Mrs. Disney would let him, we'd go fishing in the creek," recalled Clem Flickinger, who lived in the farmhouse across the road from the Disneys. "We'd catch catfish and bowheads. There was a place where the water was four or five feet deep, and me and Walt would take off our clothes and swim. In the winter, a whole bunch of us would go sledding and skating with a big bonfire to keep warm."

One day, Walt discovered a bunch of old burlap bags in the barn, cut them up, and sewed them together to make a tent. A couple of baffled farm cats were herded inside and the first Disney circus was ready to perform. He charged ten cents admission. But as Clem Flickinger noted: "You can't teach a cat much of anything." The audience left, unimpressed, and Flora Disney made her son give back the dimes.

A natural leader, Walt had a built-in follower in his little sister, Ruth, who was two years his junior and would do almost anything to keep his attention. One day, their parents were in town and Walt, then age 7, began playing with a big barrel of tar. The black, sticky substance, he explained, could be used just like paint. Walt dipped a stick into the tar and began to draw on the side of his parents' white house.

Even at the age of five, Ruth had a funny feeling about this grand idea. "Will this come off?" she asked.

"Oh, sure," Walt said, brimming with confidence.

Zigzags appeared from the end of Ruth's stick as she got into the spirit. Walt worked on a series of houses with smoke coming out of the chimneys.

Pausing to admire their work, they made an alarming discovery. The tar had dried and wouldn't budge. Trying in vain to scrape the wretched stuff away, Walt contemplated his father's wrath. With his vivid imagination, Walt could already see his dad deliberately cutting a long, thin branch off one of the apple trees and feel the sting on his exposed bottom.

Walt was reminded of his error in judgement for some while—the tar didn't come off the whole time the Disneys remained in Marceline. Years later, Walt wrote that his days on the farm steeped him in the true spirit of Missouri, a mixture of tolerance, independence, and "mulishness." But it seems equally likely that those traits were with Walt from the beginning. No one ever had

*Walt's little sister Ruth admired him greatly. She followed him everywhere—even into trouble.*

© Walt Disney Enterprises

an easy time telling him what to do. From his early childhood, he had a maddening confidence in his own opinions.

One of his strongly-held views was about school. He had started first grade a year late—at the age of seven—and staunchly resisted the notion that school could be good for him. While his teachers at Marceline's brand-new Park School droned on about arithmetic or spelling, he doodled pictures of farm animals. The most significant mark he left were his initials, carved carefully on his desk.

That desk is now behind a glass showcase in the Walt Disney School in Marceline.

# Elias

"I had a tremendous respect for my dad. Nothing but his family counted."
—WALT DISNEY

*Elias Disney*

After Walt was grown-up, he enjoyed talking about his boyhood battles with Elias. Of course, Walt always liked to tell stories with a flair—and what could be more dramatic than tales of beatings he had suffered as a boy?

In fact, Walt may have feared Elias, but in many ways, the boy was a great deal like his father. They were both perfectionists, quick to anger, stubborn, and proud. Neither feared a challenge or was derailed by a failure.

Elias's intensity and drive to succeed kept him on the move for most of his life. At a time when many Americans never travelled more than 100 miles from their birthplaces, Elias's various careers took him to Kansas, Colorado, Florida, Illinois, and Missouri. Along the way, he worked as a carpenter on the railroad line and a mailman; he bought and sold an orange grove and worked as a home contractor in Chicago.

Elias was responsible and community-spirited. He rarely drank and never smoked. He hated laziness and waste. He wouldn't tolerate dishonesty.

When he felt that one of his children had done wrong, he was likely to flail out suddenly. "Great Scott," he'd exclaim, jaw set and face red. "Land o' Goshen!" Elias's speech seemed old-fashioned to his children. But his message was clear. There was one right way to do things: his way.

The three younger children had relief from his constant demands when they were in school. But the two older sons, Herbert and Raymond, worked with him from dawn to dusk. This was a particular strain since they had never really accepted their lives as farm boys. Neighbors called them "city dudes," when they strutted along Main Street in their store-bought blue suits and stiff-brim hats. The farm meant nothing to them but backbreaking labor.

Elias didn't help matters much. He paid them nothing, believing that a family worked together for the common good. When they took jobs on a neighboring farm to make spending money, Elias insisted they use it to help pay the family's debts.

This was the last straw.

One day in 1908, Herbert secretly rode into town and withdrew the money he and Raymond had saved from the bank. Pretending to be unusually tired, the boys went to their bedroom early. They packed, hopped out the window, walked into town, and caught the 9:30 train back to Chicago.

With the older boys gone for good, Elias's hopes for the farm faded. He struggled for two more years, with Roy as his only farmhand. Then, in the fall of 1910, illness dealt the final blow to his plans. His head ached all the time; his throat felt like it was filled with burning daggers. Finally, a doctor diagnosed typhoid fever.

Walt's mother, Flora, was terrified. Typhoid fever killed tens of thousands of Americans each year. Though Elias might have been treated with medicine in a hospital in Chicago, the only treatment available to him in Marceline was cold baths to keep down the fever. But neither Walt nor Ruth knew enough to be alarmed. When Flora held orange slices up to his dry lips, the children looked on jealously. "Those orange slices looked so wonderful to me, I almost wished I was sick so I could have some, too," Ruth remembered eighty years later.

Medicine everywhere was just coming out of the Dark Ages. Scientists had only recently figured out that bacteria cause diseases like typhoid fever. The very idea that surgeons should wash their hands between operations was considered new and exciting. Doctors would move from bed to bed, feeling patients' tongues in an effort to figure out what was ailing them. So, if the patient in the first bed had typhoid fever, by the end of the week so did everybody else in the hospital.

In the Disney household, Elias's mind was filled with feverish nightmares much of the time. Then, after weeks of typhoid fever, pneumonia followed.

There was no question, Flora knew now. Even if Elias recovered—and she had faith in God that he would—he'd never be able to farm again.

When Elias got back on his feet, he and Flora decided to sell the farm and move to bustling Kansas City. Roy and Walt, now almost nine, were sent to tack up posters in all the little nearby towns to announce the auction of the Disneys' possessions. They made trip after trip to deliver the goods the family had sold. Flora heated bricks up in the oven, which the two boys placed on the floor of the buggy to keep them warm.

After the farm was sold, for $5,175, Flora and Elias rented a house in Marceline for six months so their younger children could finish the school year.

Walt would have been just as happy to get going right away. As much as he loved Marceline, moving meant adventure, new experiences, and excitement. He had already seen all the sights the small town had to offer.

It never occurred to him that his new life might make him dream of the farm he had left. Or that his days of running barefoot and carefree, king of the apple orchards, were over forever.

# Kansas City

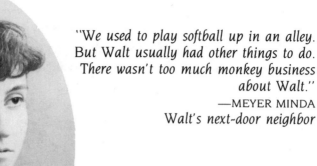

© Walt Disney Enterprises

*"We used to play softball up in an alley. But Walt usually had other things to do. There wasn't too much monkey business about Walt."*
—MEYER MINDA
*Walt's next-door neighbor*

*Flora Disney*

Soon after his family arrived in Kansas City in the summer of 1911, Walt's father invested his farm money in a newspaper route of two thousand customers. Naturally, he counted on Walt and Roy to help deliver the papers. At 3:30 A.M., while the stars were still shining brightly in the sky, Walt was joggled from his dreams. It took him two hours to distribute his backbreaking pile of newspapers in the morning and another two hours in the afternoon.

On hot summer days, in that era before air-conditioning, all the windows in the neighborhood were wide open. In the mornings, when Walt rolled the iron-wheeled newspaper cart down the concrete driveway of his Kansas City home, irate neighbors leaned out of their windows to complain about the ruckus he made. Walt told them to mind their own business. He didn't want to be there any more than his neighbors wanted to hear him.

Gone were the pigs and horses, owls and meadowlarks of Marceline. Gone were the majestic weeping willows and cool country creeks. The Disney home, at 2706 East 31st Street in Kansas City, nearly touched the neighbors' houses on both sides. The tiny backyard featured little more than a vegetable patch. In front, the house was so close to the road that the curtains were kept drawn

13

so passengers on the 31st-Street trolley couldn't see in the family's windows.

Walt snatched precious moments of fun whenever he could. Much of his newspaper route was in a neighborhood better off than his own. In the mornings, he played with the toys that well-to-do children left out on their porches: miniature cars and airplanes, carved wooden circuses and blocks. When he was finished, he placed each toy back exactly where he found it, making sure that no one would ever know that he touched anything.

Like his brothers before him, Walt worked for no pay. He had all the necessities of life, and Elias Disney wasn't about to let him spend money on frivolities.

Frivolities were exactly what Walt craved. He yearned for pennies to buy cinnamon balls, lemon drops, and caramels at the candy store; nickels for movies; dimes for sundaes and lemon phosphates at the soda fountain.

With boundless energy, he tried to earn pocket money. He delivered medicine for the local drugstore. He worked in the candy store during recess. He started a soda stand on his block with another boy. The young entrepreneurs bought their soda for two cents a bottle and sold it for five cents to the wagons and cars that passed by their stand. Then several particularly hot days hit. The boys drank their whole supply themselves and were out of business.

Walt's best hope for steady income was in selling newspapers on the streetcar at 6:30 in the morning after he had finished his regular newspaper route. He talked Elias into ordering an extra fifty newspapers. When the ever-practical Elias insisted on putting these earnings in the bank, Walt secretly ordered yet another fifty papers that he sold behind his father's back.

In between his morning and afternoon deliveries, Walt was off to the Benton School, where to his humiliation, he and his sister Ruth had been asked to repeat the second grade. This setback made little difference to her. In Marceline, she had been jumped ahead of her own age group—right into Walt's class. When Benton held her back, she was once again with children her age. But poor Walt was now more than two years older than most of his classmates. To make matters worse, he frequently slipped off to sleep. One of his teachers arranged her classroom according to performance, and he ended up sitting in a chair near the back door—the "second dumbest" seat in the room.

With rigorously scheduled days, impatient teachers, and a demanding father, Walt might have become rebellious and discouraged. But he never felt sorry for himself.

Flora Disney made sure of that.

A tall woman with high cheekbones, and deep, large, brown eyes, Flora was the heart of the Disney family. If Walt was endowed with a touch of magic, his mother was the person who wielded the magician's wand. Flora encouraged the whole family to have fun and not take themselves too seriously. "She would kid the life out of my dad when he was peevish," Roy once said.

One day, Walt brought home a mechanical practical joke called a "plate lifter." The little gadget allowed you to push down on a bulb and force air through a tube to make a plate at the other end of the table rise and fall as if by magic. "Let's pull that on your father," she suggested, grinning broadly.

Before they sat down to eat, Walt set the contraption under his father's plate and handed the other end to his mother. Every time Elias put his spoon anywhere near his soup, the bowl would move around like it was sitting on a toad. Only Elias didn't seem to notice.

"My mother was just killing herself laughing," recalled Walt. "She kept doing this and finally my dad said, 'Flora, what is wrong with you? Flora, I've never seen you so silly. . . .'"

The more puzzled her husband looked, the harder Flora laughed. Finally, she had to get up and go lie down in the bedroom. Elias never did catch on.

Flora, a former schoolteacher, held the family together. She made sure that Elias was reconciled with Herbert and Ray, who were now adults and living in the area. She loved entertaining the family's many relatives. The little nieces, nephews, and cousins who visited her home all remembered her as a wonderful playmate. "If a child was acting up, she would just divert him to something else," recalled Ruth.

Walt inherited his perfectionism and willingness to tackle something new from his father. From his mother came an ability to laugh and a down-to-earth delight in the unsophisticated, sometimes slapstick humor of human nature.

The two parents balanced each other. One gave Walt his drive, the other his sense of fun.

# Center Stage

*"Walt was enthused about everything. He was one hundred percent interested in everything he did."*
—WALTER PFEIFFER
  *Walt's best friend*

*Walt Disney,* right, *and Walt Pfeiffer*

© Walt Disney Enterprises

Though most of the teachers at Benton School thought Walt was just an unremarkable boy, in the fifth grade he astounded everyone. He memorized the Gettysburg Address for fun and came to school dressed as Abraham Lincoln. He wore his father's old coat, a homemade beard, and a cardboard top hat blacked with shoe polish. He even pasted a putty wart to his cheek.

His teacher, Miss Olson, was so impressed with his performance that she called the principal, who took him to perform in every class in the school. In the sixth grade, he was asked to repeat his Lincoln act. "Miss Olson always said I was going to be a real actor because I squinted my eyes on certain passages," Walt said proudly.

His success in performing for a crowd awoke something new in Walt. He found he loved being the center of attention. The sound of applause was absolutely intoxicating.

Happily for Walt, about this time his family moved to a bigger house at 3028 Bellefontaine in Kansas City. A few doors away lived a boy named Walter Pfeiffer, who became Walt's first truly close friend.

Walt Pfeiffer's house soon became Walt's home away from home. The Pfeiffers were a jolly joke-telling group. The large family would sit around the piano and sing. Walt ate so many meals there he began to call Walt Pfeiffer's mother "Mom Pfeiffer."

The boys shared a passion for Charlie Chaplin, who had recently emerged as a wildly successful silent film star. Every chance they got, they went to vaudeville shows where they saw singers crooning the latest Irving Berlin hit; dancers who tried to fox-trot like the nationally famous Irene and Vernon Castle; and magicians who escaped from locked trunks.

Soon, encouraged by the fun-loving Mr. Pfeiffer, the two boys started performing at Benton School every chance they got, with skits like "Fun in the Photograph Gallery." Walt Disney pretended to take a classmate's picture with a camera that squirted water in the unsuspecting victim's face. Then, when he pulled a sheet of paper out of the camera, it would be a cartoon of the person that Walt had drawn in advance.

They put together a comedy act, called, among other things, "Hans and Mike," "Pat and Mike," "The Two Walts," "Chaplin and the Count," and "Chaplin and the Cow." The boys wanted to try out their stuff in amateur-night contests held in local theaters. But Walt was sure that such silly shenanigans would infuriate his dad. Would his father let him spend his evenings on the amateur stage when he couldn't even stay awake in class?

Walt didn't want to hear the answer to that question. So he didn't ask it. "I'd go down and sneak him out of the window, so his dad wouldn't know it," said Walt Pfeiffer. "When we'd get through, we'd shove him back in the window and I'd go home."

In fact, Elias and Flora knew a good deal more about Walt's excursions than he dreamed. "They thought it was delightful," Ruth said. "They just loved it.

"One time Roy got wind that Walt was going to be in an amateur night somewhere," she recalled. "So we all hurried down to the theater and sure enough he was acting like Charlie Chaplin. According to us, he was the best. But he didn't win the prize."

On another occasion, Walt's family saw their acting son totally by surprise. As Ruth told the story, "We went to this amateur night, and the man came out and said now he's going to juggle some chairs with a boy on top. So he went back and got a chair and had a boy . . . the boy was Walt! All the family was surprised. Mother said he was as white as a ghost, three or four chairs up."

It looked for a while like Walt was going to try to become an actor or a comedian when he grew up. But as much as he loved performing, he had an unusual knack for art, as well. Mice danced up and down the margins of his books and on the corners of his school assignments. Classmates loved his pictures of Maggie and Jiggs, popular comic-strip characters. "He could draw them just as well as George McManus, the real cartoonist," said William Brown, another Benton student. "He wouldn't just copy what was in the newspaper, either." With his father's consent, Walt began taking classes at the Kansas City Art Institute on Saturdays.

Though most of his teachers at Benton School were frustrated by Walt's lack of interest in reading, writing, and arithmetic, at least one saw that there was something special about Walt and encouraged him every chance she got. Her name was Daisy A. Beck. A stylishly dressed woman in her late thirties, Miss Beck was Walt's seventh-grade homeroom teacher. She also taught mathematics and coached the track team.

Leagues of her former students remembered her as a gifted teacher who had the knack for bringing out the best in her students. A great-nephew of hers described Miss Beck as someone who treated people with "unconditional acceptance," and that was exactly what Walt needed. When he dozed in class, she understood he was exhausted and let him rest. Though he was no athlete, she urged him to try out for track. "Hop right out there at recess and show me what you can do," she said. Walt hopped. He learned how to sprint and even won a medal at the annual track meet.

She was master of the encouraging nudge. Walt had a "great mind," she told people, but he just wanted to clown around and draw. Gently, she made him do his assignments. "You've got to have something in your brain," she told Walt. "You can draw all you like—after you've finished your arithmetic work."

At 3 P.M. on Fridays, Miss Beck invited Walt to the blackboard, where he drew cartoons and captivated his classmates with stories. With a piece of chalk in his hand and the eyes of the class fixed on him, he was both actor and artist. He revelled in the attention and adored "Daisy A."

When graduation from the Benton School rolled around in June, 1917, Daisy A. was thrilled Walt had made it. It wasn't unusual for children in those days to drop out before they finished the seventh grade.

18

The big day went off without a hitch. Walt surprised his parents by delivering a patriotic speech to the assembled guests. Ruth, as the smallest one in her class, led the graduation procession. Right up until the end, Walt and another young artist named Willie were kept busy drawing pictures in their fellow students' class books.

A few of the girls hoped they would get Willie—they thought he drew better. All of which proves that seventh graders don't know everything. Willie went on to make his living reading gas meters.

# The War for Independence

© Walt Disney Enterprises

*"You can't force people to be scholars.
Everybody does not fit into that pattern.
There's other ways that people get
educated."*

—WALT DISNEY

*Walt and a friend in uniform*

Walt was free.

After six years, his grueling newspaper route was about to cease. Elias had done well, increasing the size of the route to three thousand homes. For years he had been investing his money in O'Zell Company, a promising jelly manufacturer in Chicago. Now he had word that the company was about to bring out a new soft drink to rival Coca-Cola. By selling the route, he was able to bring his investment to the impressive sum of $16,000.

With that kind of money tied up, he felt it was important that he keep an eye on the business. He moved back to Chicago to become O'Zell's head of plant construction and maintenance. Flora and Ruth went with him. Grammar school was over and a giddy Walt remained in Kansas City for the summer. He lived in the house on Bellefontaine with his oldest brother, Herbert, Herb's wife and two-year-old daughter, and Roy.

Roy looked out for his little brother. He knew Walt better than anyone else, despite the fact that they were very different. Roy had been thrust into a responsible role very early in life, when Elias took sick on the farm in Marce-

20

line. First as a son, then a brother, then a father and businessman, Roy never lost his sense of purpose. He was smart and studious, with a natural ability in mathematics. It would have surprised no one to see him stay with his current employer, the First National Bank of Kansas City, for the rest of his life, determinedly climbing the ladder of success.

Walt, by contrast, plunged through his days with a kind of oblivious ease. He was a talented artist and enthusiastic actor, but his family had no idea what he would really end up doing with his life. With his irrepressible energy, Walt was involved in more activities than any three other boys and worked harder than anyone Roy had ever seen. But he could be maddeningly careless. Walt thought nothing of borrowing Roy's clothes and returning them, spots and all, to the closet in the blind hope that he might not notice. Hardly a week went by that Roy didn't reach for one of his ties, only to find a big chili stain right in the middle. Walt was constantly and unashamedly bothering Roy for money and despite all his hard work had no sense of the value of a dollar.

With Flora and Elias several hundred miles away, Roy decided that a solid summer job might teach his kid brother some valuable lessons about responsibility. He pronounced that it would be "very educational" for Walt to sell newspapers, candy, fruit, and soda on the Santa Fe Railroad for the summer and he put up the $15 in security money that the railroad required.

Walt was a year too young to qualify. So, the fifteen-year-old started what was to become a Walt Disney tradition: He lied about his age to get the job.

"Peanuts, popcorn, newspapers," he bellowed, preening for the passengers in his blue uniform with its official-looking badge and shiny brass buttons. He loved the plush velvet compartments of the train and the nonstop tumult of the new Union Station in Kansas City. He was enchanted by the countryside roaring past as the train hurtled along. Most of all, Walt relished the opportunity to see new places.

The job was so much fun that Walt completely forgot to make any money. He allowed suppliers to shortchange him or to sell him rotten fruit that attracted flies and had to be thrown out en route. Once he left his soda bottles on a portion of the train that was detached and sent to parts unknown. Several times, he forgot to lock up his supplies, and returned to find his candy stolen.

When the summer came to an end, and Walt had to join his parents in Chicago, the train company wouldn't return Roy's $15. Walt owed them that much and more.

He wasn't concerned. His job had been heaven. It had given him his first taste of freedom.

It was anguishing to return to home and school. Life with Flora and Elias looked particularly bland to Walt this fall of 1917. For five months, the entire country had been consumed by "the war to end all wars"—that would come to be known as World War I.

Walt wanted nothing more than to "save the world for democracy." Roy joined the Navy that fall and "looked swell in that sailor's uniform," Walt said. At 15, Walt thought he was still far too young to enlist—until he was briefly mistaken for a cadet while seeing his brother off at the train station. "Come on, didn't you hear me?" the sailor in charge yelled at Walt. "I said fall in."

Walt thought, "Me? Me? My God." From that moment on he rarely stopped fantasizing about fighting in the war himself.

At such a time, who could expect a young man like Walt to care about Chicago's McKinley High School? English, physiology, and algebra seemed absolutely pointless when the civilized world was caught in a titanic struggle between good and evil.

Shoe factories were making combat boots; railroads and telegraph lines were taken over by the government for military use; families saved hundreds of tons of fruit pits—they were burned and used to manufacture gas masks.

Americans eagerly gave up bread on Mondays and Wednesdays, beef on Tuesdays, and pork on Thursdays and Saturdays to save food for the soldiers. Nothing was too difficult if it meant defeat for the German leader, Kaiser Wilhelm, and his troops.

A hysterical fear of spies and all things German abounded—"German agents are everywhere eager to gather scraps of news about our men, our ships, our munitions," warned one magazine ad. Americans no longer could refer to German measles, hamburger, or sauerkraut—they were now "liberty measles," "liberty steak," and "liberty cabbage."

Trapped in high school, Walt took refuge in the offices of the *Voice*, the student magazine, and spent his time drawing war-related cartoons.

One showed a paunchy fellow saying, "I am too fat to fight," and being told, "Why don't you stop eating so much and save food for the boys over there?" Another pictured nine jolly gentlemen in ties and jackets happily gloating over the inexplicably dead body of the German Kaiser, broken sword

© Walt Disney Enterprises

*Walt was swept away with the drama of the First World War, and his artwork turned patriotic.*

by its side. Even those that didn't have war themes included tiny signs that said, "Help Uncle Sam Win This War," or "Your summer vacation, work or fight."

Three nights a week, Walt attended the Chicago Institute of Art where he learned about anatomy and cartooning from illustrators who worked on the *Chicago Record* and the *Chicago Daily Tribune*. One of his teachers, K. C. Orr, drew a daily strip in the *Tribune* called the "Tiny Tribune,"—and Walt imitated it for the school paper with "The Tiny Voice."

During the school year, Walt also worked at the O'Zell Company. He cleaned up, ran the bottle washer, and the machine that mashed apples. Inhaling the sickeningly sweet vapors of the jelly factory was not Walt's idea of a good time. When summer rolled around, he took a job at the post office (lying about his age once again). Each day, as he sorted mail, he listened to the patriotic beat of a fife-and-drum corps in the street below, accompanied by men chanting, "Come on, you slackers. Come on up and join. We dare you."

Walt was consumed with the excitement and the glory of it all. The drama of larger-than-life men fighting for truth and justice shoved any realistic thoughts of death and destruction from his mind.

As it happened, he got a taste of the violence of war right in Chicago. One day when he was just about to leave the post office, a violent explosion rocked the building, tearing bricks loose, shattering glass, killing four men, and wounding thirty. One of the dead was a mailman who worked only two desks from Walt. Newspapers the next day graphically reported that every bone in his body was broken, and that the corpse had to be rolled onto a canvas so that it would not fall apart. Walt shuddered, realizing that he missed being in the same spot by about three minutes.

Hysterical coverage immediately placed blame for the tragedy on two sources—"German agents bent on terrorizing Chicago," and "the Industrial Workers of the World," a radical group that many people suspected of taking money from the Germans to cripple American business.

Walt tried to enlist. He tried to join the Army. He tried to join the Navy. He tried to join the Marine Corps. None would take him—sixteen-year-olds were not accepted. Then a friend told Walt about the Red Cross Ambulance Corps, an all-volunteer unit that had less stringent age requirements than the armed forces.

Two problems remained. Flora and Elias. Walt needed a passport and that meant he needed his parents' signatures. Elias adamantly refused, but finally Flora relented and signed the form for herself and her husband. Afterwards, Walt, still several months short of the minimum age, seventeen, took a black pen and carefully changed the year of his birth from 1901 to 1900. Soon he was living in a tent near the University of Chicago learning how to fix motors and drive ambulances.

Then, when Walt was almost on his way to France, he came down with the Spanish Influenza. This deadly strain of flu started in an army fort in Kansas in March, 1918, and spread through every country in the world. More than 20 million died, over twice the number killed in World War I.

When Walt was offered the chance to go home, he took it. An ambulance delivered him to his frightened mother and father. Ruth's favorite teacher had died of the flu, as had many neighbors and friends.

*Walt lied about his age to get into the ambulance corps, changing the year of birth on his passport application from 1901 to 1900.*

© Walt Disney Enterprises

For a week, Walt was delirious and ran a high fever. His mother watched over him—and later Ruth, who caught the disease. Ruth slept next to the stove and Walt took his parents' bedroom. Flora became ill, too, but she continued to nurse Ruth and Walt. Within a few weeks, all three recovered.

When Walt went back to his training camp, he was shocked to discover that his friends had shipped out. Walt wound up in another unit on its way to Sound Beach, Connecticut—the last stop on the way to France.

One of the other fellows in his unit was Ray Kroc—the man who would go on to found McDonald's. He recalled that Walt was "regarded as a strange duck, because whenever we had time off and went on the town to chase girls, he stayed in the camp drawing pictures."

Then the unthinkable happened. On November 11, 1918—the eleventh hour of the eleventh day of the eleventh month—armistice was declared, the war was over.

This was a disaster for young men like Walt. "There was a fantastic celebration in town, but my folks found me up in my room crying," said one of Walt's friends back in Kansas City. "The war was over and I didn't have a chance to get into it. I was heartbroken."

As Walt recalled, "We were so darn naive, we didn't know what it meant. We just knew that we'd missed out on something. . . ."

His bags packed and ready to go home, Walt went to sleep. At three o'clock in the morning a voice awakened him. "Up everybody! Up! . . . Fifty guys are going to France."

"Oh, I won't be one of them," said Walt, and he turned over and went back to sleep.

The next thing he knew, his pals were shaking him. "You lucky bastard," they yelled, pulling him out of bed and dumping him on the floor. "You're going." The Red Cross still needed men to help in cleanup operations. When the names were called off—Walter E. Disney had been number fifty.

By the next morning, he was out at sea on his way to France.

# Vive La France!

© Walt Disney Enterprises

*"I didn't need a cushion or a big feather bed. I didn't care where I ate. . . . Everything was an experience."*
—WALT DISNEY

The trip to France, aboard a clanky cattle boat called the *Vauban*, was the first time Walt had been on a ship. His bunk was tiny, his uniform fit badly, and men to the left and right of him were seasick with the regularity of the tides.

Walt hardly noticed. Ahead lay the excitement and independence for which he yearned.

The fact that he might have been blown into a thousand tiny pieces only added to the excitement of the trip. The *Vauban* was still carrying ammunition—and the ocean was thick with mines. "We were sleeping down there in the ship and there was a lot of TNT and everything," said Walt. "It could have blown us up any time. . . . We said, 'Gee this is thrilling! You know . . . we could get blown up.' " When the ship neared shore, it was accompanied by minesweepers—boats designed to detect mines before they went off, so they could be shot out of the water. "We were hoping they'd hit a mine, so we could see them shoot it," said Walt.

On December 4, the day before Walt's 17th birthday, his ship docked in Le Havre, where Walt had his first real glimpse of France. Immediately, he and the other men had a problem. In harbor towns like Le Havre the public rest rooms were truly public—open air urinals on the street. Walt had heard about such things, but like any good midwestern boy he wasn't about to step right up and use one. As the day of sight-seeing drew on, however, the facilities looked more and more acceptable. Finally one of Walt's buddies said, "I don't care where I am. I gotta go." After that, everyone followed suit.

Later that day, the members of the American Ambulance Corps boarded a train for St. Cyr, a small town a few miles from the palace at Versailles. Their quarters there were bleak and cold; Walt wrapped himself in newspapers at night to avoid frostbite. There was no trained chef and horribly prepared pork and beans were on the menu for dinner night after night.

The first evening in St. Cyr was one to remember. Walt was wandering around the camp when he ran into a friend who offered to buy him a drink at the local bistro. Just as they walked in, people jumped up from behind the tables and counters. "Happy birthday, Dis," they yelled. Someone had discovered that it was Walt's birthday and everyone seemed anxious to celebrate. They toasted Walt over and over again with cognac and grenadine.

Then Walt got his present: the bill. All his newfound friends disappeared into the night. The newly turned 17-year-old good-naturedly emptied his pockets to pay the tab.

Soon after, Walt was transferred to Paris where he made deliveries and chauffeured officers. When no one needed a driver, he and the other fellows sat around playing poker and smoking cigarettes. This was all great fun, and so Walt was terribly concerned when he was almost thrown out of the Ambulance Corps a couple of months later.

It all started when he and a helper were sent to deliver a load of beans and sugar to a small town a couple of hours from Paris. The truck broke down in a snowstorm three miles from their destination.

Walt and his buddy remembered their training: "Never leave your vehicle." They pushed it next to a watchman's shed by the railroad tracks. His companion headed back to Paris for help and Walt huddled in the shed with the watchman, who fed his little stove with one lump of coal at a time. Walt shared his meager supply of bread, cheese, and chocolate.

Two days passed without sleep. Another watchman replaced the first. Finally, Walt walked to town, found a restaurant, then fell deeply asleep for 24 hours.

When Walt awoke, he hustled back to the shed. His truck had disappeared! Back in Paris, he learned that his unreliable helper had been drunk for two days before he reported the breakdown and had the truck towed back.

Walt's superiors angrily told him that he could be kicked out of the Red Cross.

"They made a big thing of this," said Walt. Luckily one of the men Walt worked for came to his defense. He said, "Look, this boy sat there for two nights. What happened to the helper?" It turned out the helper was already in the brig. Much to his relief, they let Walt off with a few stern words.

Weeks later, Walt was transferred again—to a canteen near the town of Nancy that served doughnuts and coffee to soldiers and gave them a place to relax. Walt bought supplies and took his coworkers on picnics. In his spare time, he drew cartoons and sent them to humor magazines in the United States. The only sales he made were to his friends; he decorated their jackets with fake French medals and drew funny drawings of them to send to their girlfriends. For a while he was in business with a young man from Georgia, painting helmets to make it look as if they had been through battles. His friend

*No dull ambulances for Walt to drive—he decorated his with cartoons.*

© Walt Disney Enterprises

sold the helmets to GIs who wanted souvenirs. Sometimes he even shot holes through them, and pasted on a bit of human hair to make them look more authentic.

Toward the end of his stay, Walt met up with Russell Maas—the Chicago friend who had told him about the Red Cross unit. He and Russell both loved animals and they bought themselves a couple of German shepherd puppies. When Russell was shipping out, Walt gave him $75 to feed his dog and bring it home for him.

After about a year in France, Walt was anxious to return to the states. Between his pay, his artwork, and a big dice game, he had saved over $600. He and Russell had made ambitious plans for spending that money. These sophisticated men of the world were going to buy an old boat and float down the Mississippi River together with their two dogs.

# A Kansas City Star

© Walt Disney Enterprises

*"I didn't care for the jelly business."*
—WALT DISNEY

Elias was bursting with good news when Walt arrived home in the fall of 1919. Hundreds of thousands of veterans had sucked up almost every job available. But Elias had taken care of his son.

"Walter," he said, "the head of the O'Zell has a job for you down there. It will pay $25 a week."

With good news like that, Walt hardly needed any bad news. But there was plenty of that kind, too. His good friend, Russell Maas, had changed his mind about sailing down the Mississippi. Walt's German shepherd had died on the way home. A girlfriend, who had been writing to him regularly in France, informed him that she was now married.

"I don't want that kind of job," he told his horrified dad.

"Why not?"

"I want to be an artist."

It wasn't that Elias disapproved of art. It was that he disapproved of stupidity. As far as he was concerned, turning down a steady job to try to make a living as Leonardo da Vinci was downright foolish.

But Walt was adamant. Within a few weeks he was back in Kansas City at the old Disney house on Bellefontaine with Roy and Herbert, doggedly pur-

31

suing a job at the *Kansas City Star*. After he was turned down as an artist, then an office boy, and finally a truck driver, Walt hustled to the bank where Roy worked to get advice. Once again, his older brother came through, sending Walt out to the Pesmen-Rubin Commercial Art Studio, where he'd heard there was an opening for an apprentice.

Walt knew nothing about advertising. Louis Pesmen wanted to see samples: drawings of tractors, for instance, that might be used in ads for farmers. Walt brought in sketches of Parisian street scenes.

When Pesmen offered to give him a shot, Walt was so startled he forgot to ask about his salary. The first week on the job, he was afraid to get up from his drawing board, lest his new employers think he was lazy. On Friday, one of his bosses came over and said they intended to give him $50 a month. "I could have kissed him," said Walt. "I thought I was going to get fired."

Walt spent his time drawing horses, cows, and bags of feed for farm-equipment catalogues. He learned the tricks of the trade. But shortly before Christmas, sales fell off, and Pesmen explained there wasn't enough money to pay his salary anymore. Walt worked for the post office for a while but that job ended after the Christmas rush.

Then a friend from Pesmen-Rubin came to call. Ubbe Iwwerks was a quiet, gangly eighteen-year-old. The son of Dutch immigrants, Ubbe was an extraordinarily talented artist, though painfully awkward with people. A couple of years before, he had quit school and was now supporting his mother. He, too, had been laid off from Pesmen-Rubin. Though Ubbe didn't say much, it was clear to Walt that he was panicking.

"Let's go into business," suggested Walt. Even Ubbe thought this was a ridiculous idea. Six weeks in the commercial art business hardly qualified Walt to run his own show. But Walt had a knack for talking people into doing peculiar things.

The new company was initially called "Disney-Iwwerks." But that sounded like an eyeglass store. So Iwwerks-Disney it became. Walt used the few hundred dollars he had saved from the Red Cross to buy desks, drawing boards, and other equipment.

The first client was Walt Pfeiffer's father, who paid them for work on the *United Leatherworker's Journal*. In all, the business made $135 the first month—more than Walt and Ubbe had earned at Pesmen-Rubin. Still, there were expenses to pay and business was unsteady.

So, when Walt was offered a $40-a-week job at the Kansas City Slide Company, in the spring of 1920, he and Ubbe talked it over and decided he should take it. Ubbe struggled to keep the business running alone. Several months later, Walt convinced his new boss, Vern Cauger, to hire his friend.

At the Kansas City Slide Company (soon renamed the Kansas City Film Ad Company) Ubbe and Walt were introduced to a brave new world. Vern Cauger's artwork didn't just lie on a page, but jumped up and danced across a movie screen. The company made cartoon commercials for local businesses and the novelty, challenge, and excitement of animation hit the two young men full force.

Cartoons had only recently been introduced to theaters. The earliest ones, like "Gertie the Dinosaur," had astonished moviegoers only five or six years before. "The theater patrons suspected some tricks with wires," wrote Gertie's creator, animation pioneer Winsor McCay. By the time Walt got to Kansas City Slide, most of the successful cartoons were based on newspaper comic strips like "Krazy Kat" and "The Katzenjammer Kids." They were silent, black-and-white affairs. The motion was jerky and the action was repetitive and simple.

Still, it was motion—and that seemed pretty miraculous at the time. When you watch a cartoon, you are really seeing a series of still drawings, on individual frames of film. Each drawing is only slightly different from the one before it. Because these frames are projected onto a screen at a very rapid clip—24 to a second—you don't see each drawing individually. Instead, they blend into an illusion of motion.

The medium was tailor-made for Walt, combining his interests in drawing, storytelling, and mechanics. He loved exploring how cartoons worked and how they could be made better. The techniques at Cauger's company were clumsy. Little paper figures with movable joints were pinned to a sheet, then filmed for a fraction of a second, moved, and filmed again. The result was a very stiff, jerky animation.

Walt's bosses were satisfied. But Walt wasn't. In his off-hours, he analyzed the process looking for ways to improve it. First he and Ubbe simply worked out ways to bend the paper dolls' elbows and knees so that they had added flexibility. Then he borrowed a couple of books about animation from the Kansas City Library. He learned about the ways in which New York animators, like Max Fleischer, used drawings instead of cutouts. With drawings you

weren't limited by anything other than your imagination and your ability to use a pencil.

Soon Film Ad's cartoons were looking far more professional. Day after day, Walt begged to borrow a camera for more experimentation, and finally Cauger gave in. Walt set about trying to find someplace to set up a workshop.

The house on Bellefontaine, never particularly large, had become rather crowded in the summer of 1920 when Flora, Elias, and Ruth moved back in. Elias's dreams of a new soda to rival Coke had been smashed when the president of the jelly factory turned out to be a thief and the O'Zell Company went bankrupt. With Walt's parents and sister living there alongside Walt, Roy, and Herbert's family, the house was now holding eight. Only Ray, always the most remote Disney child, had left town to travel to parts unknown in Canada.

Walt began eyeing the unused space in his father's newly built garage. Elias, who never owned a car in his life, planned to rent the garage to someone in the neighborhood for a little extra cash. To his surprise, he found his first customer was his son. Walt agreed to pay $5 a month for the space, though Roy never recalled seeing any money actually change hands. From that time on, Walt was up past midnight, every night, working on his cartoons, adjusting lighting, trying new kinds of drawings, testing camera angles.

He enlisted his five-year-old niece, Dorothy, as an assistant. He made a film of her dropping a milk bottle to the sidewalk and then ran it backwards. "All the pieces came back together," she said, entranced.

As usual, Walt kept his intentions quiet. But he had big ideas. He figured that Kansas City movie theaters, which rented cartoons from animators out East, might buy some with a local twist. So, Walt made a few samples and headed out to the Newman Theater. With a healthy dose of presumption, he called his new features "Newman Laugh-O-Grams" before anyone at Newman had ever seen them.

The man in charge looked at the reel and agreed to talk to Walt. "How much will it cost us?" he asked.

Walt hadn't thought about that. "Thirty cents a foot," he blurted out. That was how much it cost him to make the film. The deal was done. Walt was stuck making Laugh-O-Grams for no profit.

*In his late teens, Walt worked hard, night and day. He hated to get up from his drafting table.* © Walt Disney Enterprises

He was delighted anyway. Any big event in the news turned up in the next week's Laugh-O-Gram; the theater's anniversary or a police-force scandal were typical fare. One cartoon showed a wacky professor who figured out wild contraptions to stop people from reading the subtitles out loud in the silent movies. One dumped them on the street, another bopped them on the head with a mallet.

Old friends from Benton School began to see Walt in a different light. People who barely recognized him before, now crossed the street for a hearty hello. "Hiya, Dis, how are you?" they began. "Say, I saw that thing down at the Newman the other day. . . ."

It wasn't quite international fame, but it's likely that no public recognition ever tasted sweeter to Walt.

# The Rise and Fall of Laugh-O-Grams

© Walt Disney Enterprises

*"I think it's important to have a good hard failure when you're young."*
—WALT DISNEY

Though Walt was wrapped up in his day job at Kansas City Film Ad and his night job making Newman Laugh-O-Grams, his life was warmed by the presence of family. Flora always had something good to eat waiting in the icebox. Ruth proudly listened to Walt's tales of triumph in animation. Roy and Herb were available for fun. With Flora at the stove, flipping flapjacks as fast as she could, the three brothers held pancake-eating contests to see who could consume the most.

In the summer and fall of 1921, everything changed. First, Herbert was transferred by the post office to Portland, Oregon. Then Roy was sent to a government hospital in Arizona after doctors discovered he had tuberculosis; the lung disease killed millions in the early years of the century.

Within days of Roy's departure, Flora and Elias accepted an invitation to join Herbert in Oregon, where their only grandchild now lived. They sold the house and moved with Ruth to Portland.

Walt took his family to the train and carried their suitcases in. Recalled Ruth, "I never knew Walt's emotions much, but he suddenly couldn't keep his face straight. He turned and left. He was clearly very upset. He knew he was going to be alone."

Walt found a rooming house and rented a small place to make his cartoons. He devoted himself entirely to his work. He advertised for other young people interested in learning the cartoon business. No pay, of course. Walt wasn't making any money on the venture himself. He promised to teach his apprentices and to share future profits. Before long he had several "employees."

Their first big project, "Little Red Riding Hood," turned out well. Walt abandoned all caution, quit his job, and started looking for investors to expand his little company. His sincere eyes, glib speech, and contagious enthusiasm convinced a number of Kansas City professionals to cough up $15,000. "I suppose it was probably illegal for me to be president of a corporation at age twenty," he later speculated. "If we ever wanted to get out of anything, I suppose we could have gone to court and claimed I was a minor."

Walt certainly wasn't behaving like a kid. He soon had an office staff and a half-dozen animators including his old friend Ubbe Iwwerks. They set up shop in a brand-new brick building in one of Kansas City's main shopping districts. All the employees were paid meager wages, but they didn't need much. In their late teens, they spent most of their time at work anyway. They began at nine in the morning, ended at midnight, and frequently spent weekends together, as well.

Walt and his staff didn't have enough time or knowledge to advertise their cartoons, rent them to movie theaters, and collect the fees. That was the job of a distributor. Over the years, Walt would use a number of companies—large and small—as distributors for his work. Those relationships were repeatedly unhappy ones.

The first deal he made was to produce a series of fairy-tale cartoons to be distributed by a small company called Pictorial Clubs. Walt took a down payment of only $100. Gullible and trusting, he had accepted on faith that the company would send him the remaining $11,000 when the series was delivered in six months.

Unfortunately, just when Walt was about to get his big $11,000 check, Pictorial Clubs went out of business. Six months' worth of work had been done for a hundred-dollar deposit.

"The company is worse than broke," wrote one of Walt's employees to his mother in October, 1922. "We are about two thousand in the hole and going in about four hundred more each week. . . . We have the business in sight

*Walt and his young staff worked slavishly, but still enjoyed clowning around in nearby Swope Park.*

© Walt Disney Enterprises

© Walt Disney Enterprises

and orders in to put this place over, but we lack the ready cash. . . . I am going to . . . possibly quit and get me something more sure."

Employees deserted Laugh-O-Grams. Walt's landlady kicked him out because he couldn't pay the rent. Walt moved into his office. At night, he slept on a bunch of old canvas he had heaped on the floor next to his drawing board.

Mostly, he ate on credit at a little coffee shop downstairs from his office. When his bill got up to about $60, Jerry Raggos, one of the owners, came to him. "Walter, we can't give you any more credit," he said. A couple of days later, Jerry found Walt in his office eating some beans out of a can and some bread that had been left over from a neighbor's picnic. Walt wasn't really so miserable—"I loved beans," he said—but he looked thoroughly pathetic. "Oh, Walter," said Jerry, with tears in his eyes. "Go down and get something to eat."

Walt breathed not a word of his situation to his family. Only Roy sensed trouble. "Kid, I haven't heard from you, but I just have a suspicion that you could use a little money," he wrote. "I am enclosing a check, fill it out in any amount up to thirty dollars."

Walt made it out for $30.

Soon, Walt was the only one left at Laugh-O-Grams, desperately trying to scrounge up cash any way he could to keep his company going. His persistence appeared to pay off when a local dentist called in December of 1922. Dr. Thomas B. McCrum wanted a short film made to teach boys and girls the benefits of brushing their teeth. Walt said he could do it for $500, and the dentist asked him to come to his office to wrap up the deal.

"I can't come tonight," said the frustrated Walt.

"Why not? What are you doing?"

"Nothing."

"Well," said the dentist, "why can't you come?"

"I haven't any shoes."

Walt had left his one pair of shoes at the shoemaker to have them repaired, but he couldn't claim them until he could pay the bill. The dentist paid the shoemaker, had the shoes sent over, and then signed the deal.

Walt soon delivered a film featuring Tommy Tucker, a boy who regularly brushed his teeth, and Jimmy Jones, who didn't. Tommy Tucker was well-kempt and happy. Jimmy Jones looked like he hadn't washed or changed his clothes in four months. Everybody loved Tommy, gave him good jobs and praise. Nobody wanted to get anywhere near smelly, snaggletoothed Jimmy. Then Jimmy started to brush, and changed his life.

The $500 Walt received for this short piece of drama got him going again. He went to work on a new idea.

"Alice's Wonderland" was to be the first in a series about a real little girl who had adventures in a land of animated characters. Walt claimed the idea was "distinctly different," though he was certainly inspired by Max Fleischer's "Out of the Inkwell" cartoons, which featured an animated clown who had adventures with flesh-and-blood people.

He did almost all the work on the cartoon himself. In May, when the cartoon was half-finished, Walt approached New York distributors with typically bright optimism. "We have just discovered something new and clever in animated cartoons!" he wrote. "It is bound to be a winner."

M. J. Winkler, the woman who distributed "Out of the Inkwell," replied that she was interested.

With a new beginning just around the corner, Walt was stifled by a total lack of funds. He needed more cash to finish the first Alice cartoon, but even his sparkling salesmanship couldn't turn on the money spigot again. His Kansas City investors had risked too much already without seeing a penny in return. Walt was beginning to look like a good-for-nothing.

Totally unable to pay his debts, or move forward on his work, Walt's company finally declared bankruptcy.

In July, 1923, Walt sold his movie camera, and headed to Hollywood with his few remaining possessions: a pair of pants, some underwear, a checkered coat, a few shirts, a frayed cardboard suitcase, and his unfinished print of "Alice's Wonderland." "I was just free and happy," he said, "I was 21 years old going on 22. . . ."

# Hollywood

"When I got to Hollywood, I was discouraged with animation. I figured I had gotten into it too late. I was through with the cartoon business."
—WALT DISNEY

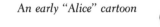

*An early "Alice" cartoon*

© Walt Disney Enterprises

When Walt arrived in California, he moved in with his Uncle Robert, Elias's stocky, cigar-smoking, 62-year-old brother who had moved West a couple of years earlier. He paid his uncle $5 a week for room and board, and spent his first days touring the big movie studios.

The early 1920s were a heady, wild time in Hollywood. Silent film stars lived in gaudy palaces, set in orange groves and vineyards. Tom Mix, the King of the Cowboys, earned more in a day than many families did in a year. Celebrities like Lillian Gish, Gloria Swanson, and Rudolph Valentino had millions of adoring fans who hung on every bit of gossip reported in the daily newspapers. Directors like Cecil B. DeMille, Erich Von Stroheim, and D.W. Griffith had the power and resources to turn their whims into reality on the screen; battle scenes were filmed with an opulence rarely seen since.

Gawking at this glamorous business from outside the studio gates were tens of thousands of would-be players. Walt was no different. The only job he found was as a movie extra. Based on his experience riding horses in Marceline when he was eight years old, he was hired as a rider in a big cavalry charge. Then it rained and the studio cancelled the attack. When filming began again, a new bunch of riders was hired. "That was the end of my career as an actor," Walt said.

Although Walt had initially given up on the idea of animation, thinking that the East Coast studios were too well established for him to compete, he now began to reconsider. His uncle was getting a little nervous that he might wind up supporting his dreamer of a nephew. Cartooning was the one thing Walt knew he could do—without actually landing a job.

He set up a slapdash workshop in Uncle Robert's garage and put together a simple reel of cartoon jokes, much like the ones he had done for the Newman Theater in Kansas City. He went to see Alexander Pantages, a highly successful owner of movie theaters and vaudeville houses.

"Mr. Pantages wouldn't be interested in this," sniffed an assistant.

"How do you know I wouldn't?" came a booming voice from nearby. It was Pantages himself. Before long, he and Walt had worked out a deal, and Walt was back in business again.

His next step was to contact M. J. Winkler, the woman who had expressed an interest in the Alice cartoon. He sent her a sample of his Kansas City work, along with the news that he was "establishing a studio in Los Angeles for the purpose of producing a new and novel series of cartoons." Those were pretty lofty words for someone working on orange crates in his uncle's garage. But they were effective.

Winkler agreed to buy six Alice cartoons from Walt for $1,500 apiece. Guiltily, he decided not to do the work he had promised for Pantages. Instead of mediocre cartoons on the cheap, he could now produce his best work.

At this point, Walt made one of the best decisions of his career. His experience with Laugh-O-Grams had taught him that he needed someone else to tend to the financial side of the business. The obvious choice was Roy, who had been moved to a hospital near Los Angeles. Throughout his illness, Roy had stayed posted on the ups and downs of Walt's career. From his sickbed, he had admired his brother's initiative and creativity, but was dismayed by Walt's "silly" deal with Pictorial Club.

When Walt visited the hospital, bubbling over with news about the Alice cartoons, Roy was easily persuaded to join him in business. Although he was still weak from his battle with TB, the next day he signed himself out of the hospital.

Roy was a highly intelligent, private man who could derive pleasure both from simple tasks like cutting the shrubbery around his house and from taking exotic, adventurous trips. In business, he might have been more comfortable as president of the Bank of Kansas City than as a Hollywood mogul. But a natural gift for finance and negotiations, a deep-seated sense of fairness, and solid midwestern common sense made him a perfect business partner for Walt. Through careers that made the two brothers closer than many married couples, it was Roy's business sense that kept the Disney company going.

Walt dreamed dreams. Roy paid for them.

Together, they launched the Disney Brothers Studio in 1923. The meager start-up money included $200 that Roy had saved from his disability pension, $500 borrowed from Uncle Robert, and $2,500 that Flora and Elias kicked in after mortgaging their Portland house.

The brothers moved into a one-room apartment together.

They bought a used camera for $200.

They rented a tiny windowless studio in the back of a real-estate office and hired a couple of assistants.

"I'll make the name Disney famous around the world," Walt told his father.

# Wedding Bells

© Walt Disney Enterprises

*"I never had any idea of getting involved with the boss. The guy didn't even have a sweater to take you out anyplace."*
—LILLIAN DISNEY

Walt joked that he wouldn't get married until he had saved $10,000. The way the 22-year-old poured money into his business, that would have meant a long life as a bachelor.

Then he hired a shy, gentle woman named Lillian Bounds who had recently moved to Los Angeles from Lewiston, Idaho. Booming Los Angeles had a population of about 600,000 at the time while sleepy Lewiston boasted under 7,000 residents. Lillian, who was staying with her married sister, Hazel, was so timid about the big city at first that she rarely left her sister's house.

One morning, a friend who worked at the Disney cartoon studio dropped by Hazel's house to ask Lillian if she wanted a job. "I took the job because I could walk to it," the future Mrs. Disney said.

Lillian's seven-year-old niece Marjorie accompanied her to work the first day so she wouldn't get lost. As the week passed, she learned how to ink and paint. This tedious process was the very bottom rung of the world of animation. Inking consisted of taking the animator's drawings and copying them onto a see-through material called celluloid so that they could be photographed one

45

at a time by special stop-action animation cameras. Painting meant adding all the shadings to the drawings.

Quickly, Lillian learned that her new bosses were operating on a shoestring. The boys—as everyone called the Disney brothers—had one outfit apiece and shared one cafeteria meal for lunch. Their poverty was slightly relieved as money began to come in from the Alice cartoons. Walt hired his first animator in February, 1924, and moved to larger quarters. He had DISNEY BROTHERS STUDIO painted on the front window. Several months later Ubbe Iwwerks was persuaded to leave Kansas City and join them. Only now his name was spelled Ub Iwerks. He had modernized.

The brothers splurged on a secondhand Ford pickup truck and Walt began driving his two inkers home at night. Lillian, who had thought Walt nice, but not promising as a romantic prospect, noticed that he always dropped his other employee off first.

She was surprised at how interested he was in her stories about life in Idaho as the youngest of ten children of a blacksmith. Her father, who had recently passed away, was a "good-time Charlie," Lillian said affectionately. When he made a little money, he bought presents for everyone.

Walt hung on every word when she told him how her pioneering grandparents had travelled across the country in covered wagons. He relished stories of the past—just as he had when he was a small boy in Marceline. "He loved Aunt Lilly's family history," Marjorie said.

Walt never accepted Lillian's invitations to meet her family. He was ashamed of his frayed brown sweater and black-and-white-checked pants. Then he and Roy bought new suits. Walt got one with two pair of pants; Roy got a suit with only one. The next day Walt asked Lilly whether he might call on her.

Hazel and her husband were entertaining friends when he walked in for the first time. Proudly, he swivelled around. "How do you like my new suit?" he asked, showing off.

"He just had no inhibitions," Lilly said. "The family liked him immediately."

The feeling was mutual. Just like the Pfeiffers in Kansas City, Lillian's family was musical. All the Bounds girls had beautiful voices and enjoyed harmonizing. Walt dropped by more and more frequently. In the evenings, Marjorie, who usually slept on the living-room couch, was put to bed in Lillian's room, so the young couple could have privacy. When Walt was ready to leave, he gently carried her to the sofa and tucked her in. "He was the only one who ever got me in that couch so that I didn't fall out," said Marjorie. "Otherwise, I would always wake up in the morning on the floor."

In December, 1924, a welcome Christmas present came from M. J. Winkler, or more precisely, from her husband, Charlie Mintz. Mintz had taken over Winkler's business, and had ordered another eighteen Alice cartoons at $1,800 apiece.

Walt bought a used car called a Moon, which he adored. It had all steel wheels, running boards, a sweeping hood, and an exposed radiator that made it look almost like a Rolls Royce from the front. He took Lillian on long drives through the California orange groves, to tearooms on Hollywood Boulevard, and to the theater.

On these rides, Walt poured out his heart to Lilly, as he called her. Charlie Mintz was making him crazy, complaining constantly about the Alice cartoons. Often Mintz held back on money he was supposed to send, which only agitated Walt even more. Week after week, Walt asked Lilly not to cash her $15 paycheck.

Roy was making Walt unhappy, too. The two brothers were together all day in the studio and all night in their small apartment. Tension abounded. Walt complained constantly about Roy's kitchen talents. Roy complained about Walt's complaining. The brothers were ready for new roommates.

The older one made the first move. For months Roy had been pining for his Kansas City girlfriend, Edna. The two had been heading toward marriage when he came down with tuberculosis. Now, after nearly four years of separation, he telegrammed Edna and asked her to come to California to marry him. With Walt as best man, and Lilly as maid of honor, the couple was wed on April 11, 1925. Edna's mom went along on their honeymoon.

A friendship between Lilly and Edna quickly developed. Physically, Edna towered over Lilly. She was several years older and more self-assured. Edna acted like a big sister with Lilly as she did with Walt. Over tea or card games, they chatted about the Disney disposition and quirks.

Plans for Walt and Lilly to get married followed soon after Roy's wedding. These were busy months, as Walt brought three more of his Kansas City pals into the studio. Just a few days before the wedding, he and Roy made a $400

© Walt Disney Enterprises

*Walt and Lilly were married in her uncle's house in tiny Lewiston, Idaho. She giggled through the whole ceremony.*

down payment on a lot at Hyperion Avenue for a new, one-story studio that would give both brothers individual offices and their family of artists a place to grow.

The wedding was on July 13, 1925, at the home of Lilly's uncle in Lewiston, Idaho. She wore a lavender wedding dress and giggled all through the ceremony ("She always giggled when she was nervous," said Marjorie). After Walt placed a wedding ring on her finger—it was white gold with a half-dozen microscopic diamonds in it—the newlyweds took the train to Portland, where Walt introduced her to Flora, Elias, Ruth, Herb, and family.

"They were very warm and friendly," Lilly remembered. "They loved him very much and wanted him to be happy so they were happy with me."

# The Production Line

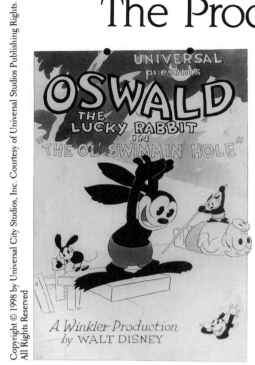

Copyright © 1998 by Universal City Studios, Inc. Courtesy of Universal Studios Publishing Rights. All Rights Reserved

*"In the early days of making these pictures, it was a fight to survive. I used to throw gags in because I was desperate. I didn't even like 'em, but I had to get one out every two weeks."*
—WALT DISNEY

Mr. and Mrs. Walter Disney settled into a tiny one-room apartment overlooking an alley. From the beginning, Lilly knew that life with Walt revolved around work. Wherever they spent their evenings—with Roy and Edna, at the theater, getting ice cream with Marjorie—she waited for the inevitable remark: "I've just got one little thing I want to do at the studio."

That "one little thing" always turned into ten or twenty. Lilly dozed on Walt's office couch while he worked. At 1:30 or 2:00 in the morning, Walt would wake her up.

"What time is it, dear?" she'd ask.

"Oh, 10:30."

The studio was madly churning out two Alice cartoons a month. There was no choice. The brothers' growing staff, largely made up of Walt's colleagues from Kansas City, needed to be paid. There were props to buy, the salary of the little girl who played Alice, fees for her teacher, for a cameraman, and uncountable other minor expenses. "An idea would come up and as fast as we'd think about it, we'd have it animated," Walt said.

One Alice followed another in a mind-numbing blur. There was "Alice

Cans the Cannibals" and "Alice Wins the Derby," "Alice Chops the Suey" and "Alice Picks the Champ," "Alice the Jail-bird" and "Alice in the Jungle." In each film, the pert little girl scampers on a very white background in the company of a large assortment of amusingly drawn, but interchangeable, dogs, cats, mice, and other cartoon animals.

Individually, the pictures were well received in the trade papers for their clever intermingling of actress and cartoon. But the gimmicky concept became harder and harder to keep fresh and funny.

Worse yet, Walt's rocky relationship with Charlie Mintz was deteriorating. The distributor was way behind on his payments. He ordered Walt to slow down production. Walt refused, and demanded his money. A bitter exchange of letters followed.

"Haven't you a single spark of appreciativeness in your whole soul?" Mintz wrote in October, 1925. "We have not made one single dollar on any picture that we have gotten from you. We have been working entirely on the prospects of what the future will bring us. . . . You should wholeheartedly be ashamed of yourself."

Added to the tension with Mintz, were the tensions Walt felt as the boss. In Kansas City, he and his employees had labored shoulder-to-shoulder, and played hard afterwards. Now his artists were still intent on playing hard— enjoying California's beautiful women and sandy beaches—while Walt was mostly preoccupied with work.

By the end of 1925, Walt no longer did much drawing himself. A perceptive judge of talent, he had decided that the other artists had greater skill than he. But this meant that he was no longer working beside them. Instead, he was directing—driving them harder than they liked.

He took on some of the characteristics of his demanding, perfectionist father. Although he was incapable, in these early years, of firing anyone, he could be abrupt and impatient, particularly since there was so much to be done and he was working all the time. He insisted they get to work on time. He forced them to do sequences over and over.

The pressures on Walt let up a bit at the beginning of 1926, when Mintz contracted for more Alice comedies. Payments were reduced to $1500 apiece, but at least they began to come on time and the battle between the Disneys and Mintz abated. Lilly and Walt moved to a larger apartment and bought new furniture; the studio opened and Walt and Roy changed the name of their business from Disney Brothers to Walt Disney Productions. A man without ego, Roy understood that it would help the company for audiences to think of a single individual turning out all the films; a man they could trust and turn to for a certain kind of entertainment.

The future looked even rosier the following year, when Universal Pictures asked Charlie Mintz for a new cartoon series based on a rabbit. Since the Alice series had clearly run its course, the Disneys were given the new project. After some false starts, Oswald the Lucky Rabbit became a quick success.

Feeling really secure for the first time since they started the business, the Disney brothers bought two adjoining lots and moved into identical prefabricated houses in the fall of 1927. Shortly afterwards, Lilly's mother moved in. Around Thanksgiving, Walt completed his family—for the time being—with a puppy. Although Lilly was inclined to think that dogs were smelly, fleabitten creatures, Walt, who adored animals, had researched the matter carefully. "I kept reading about different dogs and finally I came up with the chow," he said. "The chow does not shed hair. The chow does not have fleas. The chow has very little dog odor."

To ward off any possible protests, he hid the puppy at Roy's until Christmas, when he put it in a large hatbox, and presented it to Lilly as a gift. Lilly's scream, as the box wiggled, was memorable. But when the little chow stuck its head out, she didn't take long to fall in love.

As 1927 turned into 1928, Oswald looked more and more like a real star. Walt had a central character whose mischievous, somewhat boyish personality lent itself to the kind of physical farmhouse jokes he enjoyed.

Audiences flocked to see Oswald's latest adventures. Payments—now $2250 per picture—came on time. Every two weeks, Mintz sent his brother-in-law, George Winkler, to pick up a new cartoon, and Winkler would often stop for friendly conversations with the artists.

In February, the first contract for the Oswald pictures was up. When Walt and Lilly headed for the train to New York, they had every reason to believe that it would be renewed for a higher price. Walt was totally oblivious to any discontent among his staff. He had no idea that their friendly conversations with Winkler often turned into gripe sessions against him, or that Winkler had secretly been offering the Disney staff more money and freedom if they came to work directly for Mintz.

After the disastrous New York trip, in which Mintz told Walt he had stolen

*From childhood, Walt loved animals, and he was always trying to persuade Lilly that they needed a houseful.* © Walt Disney Enterprises

his staff and Oswald the Lucky Rabbit from him, Walt's sense of outrage and deep personal hurt were enormous. He had thought of the studio as one big happy family. The theft of Oswald was terrible, but the loss of his "friends" was a much more devastating blow.

Loyalty was a quality that Walt valued highly himself. He felt he had shown loyalty to his old Laugh-O-Gram pals when he hired them for his new business, and that loyalty had been betrayed.

Of all the animators, only quiet Ub resisted George Winkler's tempting offers. And it was to Ub that a determined Walt came with his ideas for a cartoon mouse.

# Mickey

© Walt Disney Enterprises

*"Mice? Who wants mice?"*
—A REPRESENTATIVE OF
UNIVERSAL PICTURES

*From "Steamboat Willie"*

The actual birth of Mickey took place in secret. With the traitor animators still at the studio finishing an Oswald film, Walt and Ub could only discuss the mouse in whispers or behind closed doors.

Like the mice in the Alice comedies, Mickey had round, oversized black ears, skinny arms and legs, and a long, stringy tail. Working together, Ub and Walt rounded out his form, added humanizing details (like shoes, and shorts with prominent buttons) and refined his personality. In those gloomy days, when the future of the studio was in doubt, they made Mickey an optimistic, determined little mouse. The resemblance to Walt was striking. "Walt and Mickey were so *simpatico* they almost seemed like they had the same identity," said Lilly.

Recent news stories provided the inspiration for Mickey's first adventure. Only months before, Charles Lindbergh had excited the world with the first solo airplane trip across the Atlantic. What could be funnier, Walt and Ub agreed, than Mickey dressing up like the international hero and swooping through the skies with his gal, Minnie?

Once the story was worked out, Ub worked at a blinding pace to make over

8,000 separate drawings. If another animator entered the room, Ub hurriedly threw Oswald drawings on top of his Mickey work. Each night, Walt snuck the drawings out of the studio and whisked them home, where Lilly, Hazel, and Edna were drafted as inkers and painters.

Previewed before a Hollywood audience in May, 1928, the six-minute cartoon, called "Plane Crazy," was received with laughter and applause. By this time, the other animators had departed to work for Mintz, and Walt and his tiny crew quickly made another Mickey short, "Gallopin' Gaucho." When the cartoons were finished, he confidently notified distributors that a series based on the mouse's adventures was ready for nationwide sale.

This news made a dull thud in the world of animation. Trying to sell an absolutely unknown character was just about impossible. "They don't know you and they don't know your mouse," said one distributor cynically.

Walt was stuck with two finished cartoons and no place to sell them. But what about a mouse that talked? Wouldn't that set the animation world on end? Months before, the silence of the silver screen had been broken by a Warner Brothers' film, *The Jazz Singer*. Audiences were stunned when Al Jolson opened his mouth on the screen and songs came out.

By the summer of 1928, most observers realized that sound was the wave of the future, but there were still enormous obstacles—studios had to be re-equipped, movie theaters rewired. Many people chose to take a wait-and-see attitude, letting others work out the technological problems before plunging in themselves.

Not Walt. He saw clearly that sound was revolutionizing the industry. Instead of standing back while others experimented, Walt's intuition told him that it was vital to lead the pack.

Quickly, he and his staff began work on a new Mickey cartoon named "Steamboat Willie," with scenes that lent themselves to the addition of sound. Other cartoon-makers had experimented with background music, but in "Steamboat Willie," Walt wanted the sound to genuinely add to the story, to become an important part of the whole cartoon.

He tried out a rough version of the cartoon on Lilly, Edna, and some friends in a small room at the studio. "A couple of my boys could read music and one of them could play a mouth organ," Walt said. "We . . . arranged to pipe their sound into the room where our wives and friends were going to see the picture."

© Walt Disney Enterprises

*With the daring flight of Charles Lindbergh fresh in the public's mind, what could be funnier than Mickey and Minnie cavorting in the air in "Plane Crazy"?*

Things didn't go smoothly at first. Walt and his crew couldn't get the sound matched with the action taking place on the screen. But finally the film rolled without a major hitch. Whistling sounds seemed to come right out of Mickey's mouth. When the mouse turned udders, teeth, and tails of barnyard animals into musical instruments, it really sounded like he was playing "Turkey in the Straw." Grunts, squeaks, and groans came in right on cue.

The little audience thought it was wonderful. A man not given to over-statement, Ub Iwerks reported years later, "I've never been so thrilled in my life. Nothing since has ever equalled it."

Walt's reaction? "It was terrible, but it was wonderful! And it was something new!"

Soon, Walt was heading East to arrange a recording session. Carefully, he and his staff had marked the music for "Steamboat Willie" so that musicians could see where every note fell in the action of the cartoon. Simple as that may sound, no one had ever done it before.

The scene that greeted him in New York was chaotic. Dozens of movie studios were scrambling to convert to sound. Few had the proper equipment and fewer still had figured out how to use it well. After a demonstration of sound at RCA, Walt was appalled. "My gosh—terrible—a lot of racket and nothing else," he said.

Evenings, Walt sat in his four-dollar-a-night hotel room writing letter after letter to Lilly. Long-distance phone calls were terribly expensive, but he couldn't resist. After one conversation, he wrote his wife. "I was so excited I could hardly talk. . . . I almost cried after I hung up. . . . Know how much it cost? Thirty-one dollars and fifty cents. We talked eighteen minutes. A dollar seventy-five per minute. It was worth it."

Then . . . salvation. Just when Walt was at his lowest, he met a man named Pat Powers who seemed to know every big name in the film business. Powers had his own sound equipment—and his price was much better than that of the big companies. A "big, lovable, friendly Irishman," Powers treated Walt royally, spending hours with him, showing off his many "friends" in the industry. "Powers is a very big and influential guy," Walt wrote home, completely snowed. "He is personally taking care of me."

Powers arranged for a recording studio. He convinced Walt to hire thirty musicians at $7 an hour each, four sound-effects men and a well known conductor. The beginning of the recording session did not fill Walt with hope. The bull-fiddle player showed up clutching a bottle of whiskey. The conductor insisted that Walt's bizarre marks on the film and the music were unnecessary.

While the musicians rehearsed, Walt nervously watched the clock and added up his costs.

Recording began. The bull-fiddle player drowned out the rest of the orchestra and was sent to play in the hall.

Recording began again. The orchestra sounded great. But when the film stopped running, the musicians were still playing. They hadn't kept the beat.

Expensive minutes ticked by. They tried again. They lost the beat again.

Walt's job was to do the vocals—Mickey's voice, a few squeaks, a "Yoo-hoo" from Minnie, and a parrot yelling "Man overboard." He got so excited he coughed right into the microphone and ruined another reel.

By the end of the session, Walt had spent $1,200. Not one piece of usable work had been produced.

Pat Powers had assured Walt that he would pay for the expense of a second

session, if one was needed. Now, Walt's charming new friend forgot his promise. Walt was once again stuck with the bill.

He telegrammed Roy, who set out to raise more funds. Unable to find
another way, he sold his brother's beloved Moon car. Back in New York, Walt
took control. He got rid of the bull-fiddle player and some other musicians.
He cut one of the sound-effects men. Most important, he finally talked the
conductor into following the marks on the film and music. The second recording session went smoothly. With a usable print of the film in hand, Walt's
spirits were high.

Temporarily.

Distributors told him they liked his new sound cartoon—but not enough
to buy it. "By gosh, it got laughs," Walt later said, "but I was getting the
brush-off."

Finally, Walt received some genuinely good advice from Harry Reichenbach, a famous publicity man and manager of New York's Colony Theater.
Reichenbach had seen "Steamboat Willie" and loved it. He told Walt he
wanted to run it for two weeks in his movie theater. Walt was concerned that
distributors would want it even less after it had already been introduced to the
public.

"No," said Reichenbach. "These guys don't know it's good *until* the public
finds out." Walt agreed. He received $1,000 for two weeks from Reichen-
bach—the most anyone had ever been paid for a cartoon on Broadway.

Reichenbach's instincts were right.

"Clever is a mild word to use in describing 'Steamboat Willie,' " wrote
*Weekly Film Review*. "An ingenious piece of work with a good deal of fun,"
said the *New York Times*. "It's a peach of a synchronization job. . . ." added
*Variety*.

People flocked to the Colony Theater, not to see the film—a long-since-
forgotten movie called *Gang War*—but to see the Disney cartoon.

Harry Reichenbach was right. Now that the public had spoken, the so-called
experts who made their living distributing cartoons finally knew what to think.

# Betrayed Again

© Walt Disney Enterprises

*"After every darn success there was somebody raiding me."*
—WALT DISNEY

*From "The Band Concert"*

Mickey was a hot little mouse, and Walt was suddenly an important man to the cartoon distributors of New York City. Loyally, he agreed to allow his good friend Pat Powers to distribute the cartoons. Powers claimed he only wanted to use Mickey to help sell his sound equipment. Out of every dollar that Mickey Mouse brought in, he'd take just ten cents. After that, Powers would send all the remaining money directly to Walt and Roy.

"I couldn't see that there'd be any complications in that," said Walt, delighted at the $2,500 he received when he signed the contract.

Still in New York, Walt was joined by Carl Stalling, a musician friend from Kansas City, who wrote music for three other Mickey Mouse pictures—"Plane Crazy," "Gallopin' Gaucho," and "Barn Dance." They shared a hotel room, and together added the sound tracks to the new cartoons. Then Walt returned home to Lilly and Roy in triumph.

Roy was dubious about the contract's terms. The brothers had no way to check up on Powers; they had to trust that he was honestly giving them their share of Mickey Mouse's profits. Even worse, in the contract's fine print, Walt had agreed to pay for the use of Powers' sound equipment at the staggering price of $26,000 a year.

Walt brushed Roy's concerns away, annoyed that his brother seemed to see the negative side of everything. He had been entirely charmed by the jovial Powers, who had extended welcoming arms to Walt when everyone else was turning him away.

As far as Walt was concerned, the future was golden. The studio hired four top animators, and a number of trainees, fresh from art school, had joined the staff. By the end of 1929, ten new cartoon shorts had Mickey battling cats, tap dancing on pianos, running a smiley-faced train, confronting ghosts, and rescuing Minnie at sea. Ub, whose loyalty was rewarded with a 20 percent share in the studio, was given featured billing on the credits.

Mickey fever rapidly spread. His squeaky voice—supplied by Walt—became the most recognizable in the United States. In the fall of 1929, one enterprising movie house started a Mickey Mouse Club for local children. Hundreds of others followed. Walt and Ub launched a newspaper comic strip. Carl Stalling wrote Mickey a theme song, called "Minnie's Yoo Hoo!" ("I'm the guy they call little Mickey Mouse, Got a sweetie down in the chicken house . . .") that catapulted to national popularity.

Having fathered a star, Walt might have allowed himself to relax a little. But he didn't. Now that he was on top of the cartoon heap, he wanted to change the face of the whole world of animation.

Walt plunged with enthusiasm into an entirely new series of artistic cartoons that wouldn't rely on gags or cute characters as almost all his competitors did. These *Silly Symphonies*, as he called them, generally would be set to classical music. They would stretch the limits of creativity, giving his animators a chance for endless experimentation.

Within months of his return from New York, he, Ub, and Carl Stalling had started work on the first *Silly Symphony*. Called "The Skeleton Dance," the idea was suggested by Carl, who recalled the fun he had playing with a twenty-five-cent dancing wooden skeleton when he was a child. A rather gruesome affair, the cartoon is a sort of boneyard ballet with skull-headed creatures tapping and twirling through a graveyard on a moonlit night.

Powers claimed he couldn't sell "The Skeleton Dance" anywhere. "More mice," he demanded. Remembering Reichenbach's advice, Walt convinced a Hollywood theater to give "The Skeleton Dance" a try. The public liked it

© Walt Disney Enterprises

*Experimentation continued in the studio with "The Skeleton Dance," the first of the* Silly Symphonies.

and Powers was obliged to distribute the *Silly Symphonies*. They were met by critical raves.

Once again, Walt had the familylike studio he wanted. Night meetings were common. The tension of long days of work was relieved by bridge games or badminton. In off-hours, Walt and Lilly, Roy and Edna would get together with Ub and his wife to play cards.

Walt adored the teamwork at his growing studio. Just as in Marceline, where farmers worked together building fences, harvesting the fields, and killing hogs, animation was, by its nature, a community activity. Everyone contributed gags and story ideas. The top animators drew hundreds of key scenes for a picture and the underlings—some of whom were appropriately called in-betweeners— filled in the many drawings that connected them. Putting music and art together required close collaboration and patience. In Walt's view there were no stars in this universe, only team members working together to make each picture better than the last.

It was difficult for many artists to put aside the desire for individual achievement in favor of the team approach. Ub, for one, found it hard to let others contribute drawings to a work that he was proud of—like "The Skeleton Dance." He also resented the frequency with which Walt intruded to change something on his drawing board.

Curiously, money was still a problem. That puzzled Roy. Mickey Mouse was a national phenomenon, drawing people into theaters from Hollywood, California, to Hollywood, Florida. The *Silly Symphonies* were taking off as well. Yet the checks from Pat Powers arrived infrequently and were smaller than expected.

In late 1929, Roy went to New York to see what was happening. He quickly found what everyone else in New York's film business had long known; Pat Powers didn't have an honest bone in his body. He stubbornly refused to show Roy his financial books.

"Walt," Roy said when he returned home, "that Powers is a crook. He's a definite crook. I can't find out what we've got coming to us."

Walt didn't want to believe Roy. He accused his brother of being overly suspicious. "You don't believe in people," Walt said.

"All right," Roy retorted, "you go back and find out for yourself."

Walt and Lilly went to New York in January to talk to Powers in person. Roy sent a lawyer along.

It was a wise move. Walt went alone to his first meeting with Powers, and found himself living a replay of his awful experience with Charlie Mintz. Now that Mickey was a smash, Powers wasn't content with his old deal. He wanted to make Mickey Mouse his own.

He thought he had Walt trapped. He knew the Disney brothers were short on cash. He had been purposely withholding the Disneys' profits. Now, Powers offered Walt $2,500 a week—$130,000 a year—to give up his own operation altogether and come work for him. In 1930, the president of the United States only made $75,000.

Powers didn't understand Walt. No amount of money would convince him to give up his own operation. The only reason he wanted money in the first place was to run his own shop. Stubborn to the core, the harder you pushed him, the more resolute he became.

When Walt turned the offer down, the crafty Powers moved on to Plan B. He told Walt that he had already arranged a separate deal with Ub to set him up in his own company for three times his salary at Disney. Anxious for artistic independence and for greater financial security, Walt's once staunchly loyal colleague had accepted. Powers showed Walt a telegram from Ub that confirmed what he was saying.

Walt couldn't believe it. Not again. Ub was a friend. They had grown up in the business together. It was impossible.

"Pick up the phone," Powers told him, "and call out there. Your brother knows about it now. Call."

When Powers realized how upset Walt was, he tried to soften the blow. After all, Powers didn't really want Ub Iwerks nearly as much as he wanted Walt Disney. He was just maneuvering. "Don't get upset. You haven't lost him. You can still have him. All I want is a deal," he told Walt.

Walt was unbending. "No, I wouldn't want him," he said. "If he feels that way, I could never work with him."

Back home in California, Walt faced another disappointment. Composer Carl Stalling saw the departure of Ub Iwerks as a death knell for the studio and announced that he would be leaving, too. His work had brought him plenty of offers from other cartoon executives who warned him that Disney was destined to go under. "Everybody said Walt was a failure, but I realized later that it was just a trick, that they just wanted to break Walt," Carl told *Comix Journal* years later.

© Walt Disney Enterprises

*Teamwork was the studio byword—at work and off. Mugging from left to right are Walt, Ub Iwerks, Rudolf Ising and Hugh Harman.*

Both men eventually returned to work at Disney—Carl came back for a short time, on a free-lance basis, several years later. Ub rejoined the Disney studio in 1940 and worked there the rest of his life.

But in 1930, Walt was stung and shaken by the departure of his good friends. He had such faith in his enterprise that he couldn't understand how others could give up.

Although he was personally devastated by the news, professionally the departure of his colleagues made little difference. They had jumped ship just before the studio reached commercial success. In fact, Ub's decision to return his 20 percent share of the company for $2,920 must be ranked as one of the worst business decisions of all time.

Although it cost them a bundle to break their contract with Powers, the Disneys did so and signed a new, much more profitable one, with Columbia Pictures.

Walt did learn a lesson, however. Never again would he allow his employees to have the visibility that he gave Ub and Carl. It made him too vulnerable to talent poachers.

From then on, the team approach was adhered to religiously. One name was primarily associated with the studio's product and that name was Walt Disney.

# Picking Up the Pieces

*"I worry more when things are going good than when I'm right in the middle of a fight. When everything's going good, I worry that something's going to blow up any minute."*
—WALT DISNEY

By most measures, Walt was a success. "Old Man Mickey Mouse," as one newspaper columnist dubbed the 29-year-old Walt, was already becoming a legend. The financial footing of the studio was vastly improved now that the brothers were getting the money due them. By the beginning of 1931, Walt Disney Productions had 75 employees and was still growing.

That year was probably one of the worst of Walt's life.

He had forgotten how to relax. Sleep was a luxury he denied himself. Almost every night, Lilly drowsed on his office couch while he prowled around the studio, a lit cigarette in hand. He was frustrated by the need to retrain experienced artists so they could come up to his standards. He was short-tempered when they failed, and crushed more than one fragile ego in the process.

A future of glorious possibilities stretched ahead of Walt. But emotionally, he felt embattled and confused. Desperate to get his bearings, he turned to the past. He was oddly drawn to the pile of letters that poured into the office from people who had known him before his success. He wrote to McKinley High School and the *Marceline News*. He began a warm correspondence with

65

J. M. Cottingham, his principal at Benton School, and inquired with genuine interest and affection about his favorite teacher, Daisy Beck. When a Red Cross supervisor sent him a letter and her picture, he was thrilled that she remembered him, and sent the photograph back so *she* could autograph it.

None of Walt's letters give any indication that he was on shaky emotional ground. But he couldn't seem to get rid of his unfamiliar feelings of despair. "In 1931, I went all to pieces," Walt recalled when he was interviewed by *Saturday Evening Post* writer Pete Martin. "I kept expecting more from the artists and when they let me down I got worried. . . . I got very irritable. I got to a point that I couldn't talk on the telephone. I'd begin to cry at the least little thing. . . ."

The studio's new distributor, Columbia Pictures, only added to Walt's tension. President Harry Cohn was the most difficult man in Hollywood. As director Frank Capra wrote in his autobiography, "Cruelly and stupidly, he badgered and bulldozed (Walt)."

Even Walt's generally placid home life was a source of worry. Lilly had gotten pregnant twice, and had two miscarriages. He and Lilly grew frustrated at their inability to have a baby. The birth of Roy's son, Roy Edward Disney, in January of 1930, only increased Walt's desire for a child of his own.

When Walt went to see his doctor the prescription was simple: Exercise more, work less, and get away from the studio. Roy persuaded Walt to take a vacation.

In the fall, Walt and Lilly left California for a "gypsy jaunt" around the country. They visited Washington, D.C., Florida, Cuba, and finally took a 5,000-mile cruise from Havana back to Los Angeles. "We had the time of our life," Walt said. "We met a lot of wonderful people going through the canal. It was warm and relaxed."

For the exercise part of Walt's prescription, he bounced from one activity to another. First he tried wrestling, but he didn't care to "stay for ten minutes in somebody's crotch. . . ." Boxing followed. Then golf. For a while, Walt got up to play before dawn so that he could get to the studio on time. But he'd get so furious when he missed a stroke that it didn't have the desired relaxing effect. Finally, he hit upon horseback riding, which led to polo.

Walt loved the horses, enjoyed the game, and became a fair amateur. After a few years, he joined the ritzy Riviera Club, and played with celebrities like Spencer Tracy and Will Rogers. At the same time, he all but insisted that

*Walt took up polo to relax his jangled nerves. Then he decided that the men who worked for him should take up the sport, too.* © Walt Disney Enterprises

many of the men closest to him in the company take up the sport as well.

Having followed the doctor's orders, Walt was convinced that he was cured. This painful interlude taught him that he had to let up, at least a little, and learn how to unwind. Although he would occasionally forget that lesson in the future, he never again drove himself to the point of psychological collapse. His "nervous breakdown" as he called it, passed as quickly as it came. By 1932, he was his optimistic old self and ready for a new challenge.

# Breakthroughs

© Walt Disney Enterprises

*"I've you always had a feeling that any time can experiment, you ought to do it. Because you never know what will happen."*
—WALT DISNEY

By 1932, the Great Depression had stolen the jobs of over 13 million Americans. The stock market crash of late 1929 and the upheaval that followed did not disappear like a bad dream in the morning, as President Herbert Hoover had hoped. But the Depression didn't cause any hunger pains among the men running Hollywood's movie studios. Desperate for a little relief from their trying times, Americans continued to flock to the movie theaters in search of a couple of hours of fantasy. Horror films like *Frankenstein* and *Dracula* were extremely popular, as were gangster movies and freewheeling comedies starring the Marx Brothers, W. C. Fields, and Walt's longtime hero, Charlie Chaplin.

The Disney studio prospered. Pluto and Goofy—who started life as Dippy Dawg—had arrived to join Mickey and Minnie. The two mice had become international stars with fans throughout the world. The studio had abandoned Columbia and Harry Cohn and found a more comfortable, and profitable, home with United Artists.

Money worries were further eased for the Disney brothers when they made a deal with a prominent Kansas City advertising man to handle the merchandising of Disney products. Herman "Kay" Kamen, a likeable 40-year-old with an enormous nose, heavy glasses, and a protruding chin, became a good friend of the Disney family. The arrangement, a fifty-fifty split of profits, was a happy one for both parties. Through Kamen, Walt and Roy were able to make sure that only "quality" products were sold under the Disney name—something that had troubled them in the past. Otherwise, Kamen had a free hand and he soon had Mickey and Minnie covering the shelves of department stores across the land. Their grinning faces appeared on hairbrushes, alarm clocks, napkins, phonographs, caps, socks, shoes, slippers, garters, mittens, aprons, bibs, rain capes, dollhouses, jack sets, sheets, wallpaper, and pajamas.

Then, just as Roy was finding it easier to pay the bills at the end of each month, Walt found a way to put them in debt again.

For months, Walt had attentively watched blurry and unsuccessful attempts by filmmakers to introduce limited color. You could have orangey-red and blue green and that was about it. Then Walt heard that a new company, called Technicolor, had made a breakthrough that expanded the range of colors available and provided them in vivid and clear tones.

When Walt saw the process, he became obsessed with the idea of adding color to his cartoons. Halfway through production of a new short called "Flowers and Trees," he announced that he must have it—in spite of the extreme expense.

This made no sense to Roy. His reasons for holding back were perfectly understandable in light of his brother's recent breakdown and the continuing chaos of the past nine years. He argued that color was still highly imperfect and untested. What if the color paints chipped off the cels? Or faded? Did it make sense to pioneer this experimental process when they were in the middle of a series of cartoons that was already sold? After all, United Artists and the public were completely satisfied with the product as it was and wouldn't pay a penny more for color.

Walt argued that if they kept improving their cartoons, the profits would eventually follow.

It was a typical battle in which Walt's daredevil intuitiveness and Roy's conservative desire for guarantees clashed. When Walt wanted to gamble their hard-earned money, both Disney tempers erupted in loud voices, set jaws, and waving hands.

"Roy's great ambition in life, I suppose, was to stay out of debt," said John

Hench, a longtime Disney employee. "And it was Walt's method in life to keep Roy constantly in debt."

Explosive as they may have been, the battles were always private. "Look, that's my brother you're talking about," Walt once berated someone who complained about Roy. "If I have a disagreement with him, that's between my brother and me. You're not involved in it. Don't ever let me hear you say anything against my brother again."

Walt's loyalty to Roy wasn't only born out of brotherly love. He understood that Roy's conservative nature, as annoying as it may have been at times, was crucial to the company. Roy's reluctance often forced the younger brother to develop ideas further. When Walt did so, Roy almost always came around.

In this case, Walt explained to the people at Technicolor that his brother was against color. He told them that he could only convince Roy to sign up if he was guaranteed that no other cartoon-maker would be able to use the same process for two years. Technicolor agreed and the Disneys signed an exclusive contract. Now, the *Silly Symphonies* would stand out from the competition like a rainbow in a cloudy sky. (Mickey Mouse cartoons would not get color for another three years.)

The story of "Flowers and Trees" was simple. Two trees—a handsome boy-tree and a lovely girl-tree—fall in love. But the boy-tree must battle a mean old bully-tree who is after the same girl-tree. The bully sets the forest on fire, but winds up killed himself. It rains, the fire ends, and the trees marry.

Though the story was a bit odd, the color made the film a feast for eyes accustomed to only black-and-white. Not only was the color used in the obvious ways—blue sky, green grass, red flowers—but it also helped get across changing emotions.

Walt won an Academy Award for "Flowers and Trees" in November of 1932, as well as a special award for the "creation of Mickey Mouse." In the eyes of his profession, he had achieved the greatest honor and recognition possible.

Artists flocked to the company. Many were willing to work for next to nothing just in order to have a job during the Depression. Walt added more buildings to the studio. Then, he worked on improving his staff. "I felt like if I was going to get anywhere," he said, "it was by training my own people."

A year before, Walt had arranged for his artists to take classes at the Chouinard Art Institute across town. Now, he hired instructors from Chouinard to

*Every cartoon was worked out in great detail on a storyboard before animation began. Here, Donald the chef gets into his usual share of mischief.*

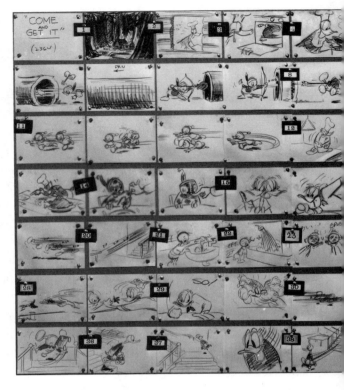

come to the studio several nights a week. The few artists who balked at putting in extra hours at their easels didn't last long at Disney. Mostly Walt's crew was happy to have the opportunity to learn.

But artistic technique alone wouldn't keep audiences in their seats. Walt had to strengthen his stories. This simple idea was of vital importance. In the early 1930s, most popular cartoons were little more than a string of gags and a lot of action. Bosko, a Mickey Mouse lookalike from Warner Brothers, just bounced from one funny situation to another, often repeating the same jokes—like splitting into a bunch of tiny Boskos after falling from a high place.

Flip the Frog, which Ub Iwerks created after leaving Disney, was no better. The Van Beuren Studio didn't even bother to make its Cubby Bear look the same from one cartoon to the next. "One design . . . made him look like a manufactured doll—the 'dead eyes' effect most animators tried to avoid," wrote Leonard Maltin in *Of Mice and Magic*.

The development of storyboards at the Disney studio was the key to stronger

© Walt Disney Enterprises

plots and characters who behaved consistently. These were five-by-seven wooden boards on which huge sheets of paper were placed. Then hundreds of sketches, drawn like an enormous comic strip, took the viewer through the cartoon in detail. Walt fiddled compulsively with storyboards. He—and others—added action, wrote new jokes, and threw out whole sections. Sometimes Walt made the writer start from scratch.

Detailed portraits of Disney stars were written—and adhered to. Mickey Mouse, for instance, "is not a clown . . ." according to one studio description. "He is neither silly nor dumb. . . . His age varies with the situation. . . . Sometimes his characteristic is that of a young boy, and at other times, as in the adventure type of picture, he appears quite grown up. . . ."

Walt's artists were assigned to draw the same character over and over, just like human performers who repeat the same roles. In fact, animators really are actors of a sort. But unlike stage or movie actors who use their voices and bodies, animators use their pencils. "You're giving a performance in the character that you're asked to draw," said Marc Davis, an artist who joined the studio in the mid-thirties. "You put yourself inside this dog or this mouse or whatever it is, and then it becomes alive. If something growls, you better growl yourself."

"More than anyone in the cartoon business, Walt understood the need to give his characters personality," said artist and writer Bill Cottrell.

Walt's drive for story and personality development paid off in 1933 with the "Three Little Pigs." With the Depression deepening, the story was especially powerful. Millions of Americans felt like the Big Bad Wolf might huff and puff their house down at any minute—so they cheered when the pigs sang "Who's Afraid of the Big Bad Wolf?"

One movie house in New York kept "Three Little Pigs" playing for so long that they put whiskers on the picture of the pigs in front of the theatre. The longer they stayed there, the longer the whiskers grew.

The film, which won another Academy Award for Walt Disney was as much a breakthrough, in its way, as "Flowers and Trees." Although it only ran about eight minutes, it had all the qualities that Walt wanted when he started the project—depth, feeling, a moral, and plenty of personality. "It got a certain recognition from the industry and the public," Walt said, "that these things could be more than just a mouse hopping around."

# Daddy

© Walt Disney Enterprises

*"I presume I'll be as bad a parent as anybody else. I've made lots of vows that my kid won't be spoiled but I doubt it. It may turn out to be the most spoiled brat in the country."*
—WALT DISNEY
*Letter to Flora*

*Walt and Diane*

Walt had been rehearsing for the job of parent for years. No matter how many hours he put in at work, he always had energy for his family. Even though he had no children of his own, relatives were in abundance. Sunday barbecues at Roy's house were a regular occurrence. Since Herb and Ray had both moved to Los Angeles, all four Disney brothers were usually in attendance. Walt and Lilly also went on special outings with their nieces, Herb's daughter, Dorothy, and Hazel's daughter, Marjorie. Ice cream was usually the goal and Sunnee, the dog, always came along and received her own cone.

As a child who had yearned for toys he could never own, Walt wanted to make sure no children he knew would ever feel the same way. So, young nephews, nieces, and children of friends received a steady supply of toys. "Aunt Lilly made me clothes for my dolls," said Marjorie. "And Uncle Walt gave me skates and scooters and all the exciting things."

He was generous in big ways as well as small. When it was time for Dorothy's first prom, her gown was a present from Uncle Walt. He sent Bill Papineau, a nephew of Lilly's, through college. He eventually hosted and paid for Marjorie's wedding and gave her a trip to Europe.

His relationship with Marjorie was a particularly close one. In 1930, she and her mother, Hazel, who had recently been divorced, moved in with Walt and Lilly. Walt loved playing the father role. If Marjorie was late, he'd be peering down from the top of the stairs when she opened the door. Marjorie started boarding school when she was fifteen years old, in 1932, and Walt insisted that she spend time with the family on weekends home. "Why'd you come home if you're not going to be here with us?" he asked.

Nothing, of course, could substitute for having children of his own. Each time Lilly was pregnant he was thrilled, then shattered when she miscarried. Finally, in mid-1933, Lilly's third pregnancy appeared to be a healthy one.

"Lilly is partial to a girl baby. . . ." Walt wrote his mother in September, 1933. "Personally, I don't care—just as long as we do not get disappointed again."

Three months later, he wrote his mother: "The big event . . . is not very far off. The doctor says Lilly is in perfect condition and everything is okay, and within another week or so everything will be over—except the crying!"

On December 18, Walt was getting an award from, appropriately enough, *Parents* magazine. In the middle of the ceremony at the studio, someone handed him a note. As the audience looked on with questioning faces, Walt bolted from the room without a word.

His baby was on the way. He hustled to the hospital and reached Lilly in time. Her last memory before going under anesthesia was the sound of Walt's nervous cough.

Within hours Diane Marie Disney was born.

The studio went wild. Roy and Edna were delighted. Marjorie, away at boarding school, reported that the entire floor of her dormitory cheered when she got the news.

From all reports, Diane was an adorable baby and Walt was a doting father from the start. The "Three Little Pigs" provided the cash for him to build a two-story English Tudor house with a pool carved out of the mountain rock. The top floor contained a plush nursery. For Christmas, the two-story-high living room accommodated a giant tree that touched the ceiling. When Diane was just a year old, she sat under this grand, sparkling tree, surrounded by toys of every size and description.

Walt immediately wanted more children. But another miscarriage after Diane's birth ended the Disneys' hopes of bearing another child. Instead, several years later, they decided to adopt, and in January, 1937, two-week-old Sharon Mae Disney was brought home to welcoming arms. "She was a very wanted child," Diane later said.

The adoption was rarely, if ever, discussed outside the family, and inside, Walt and Lilly loved and treated both children alike. As Walt explained, in simple terms, to Diane when she was five, "There are two ways to have babies. You have them yourself or you can adopt them."

In the tradition of well-to-do families of the time, the girls had a nurse. After Hazel remarried and moved out, another of Lilly's sisters, Grace, moved in and was always around to stay with the girls when the couple was out late or away on trips.

The Disney girls were oblivious to Walt's fame. At home, he acted no different from any other adoring father. He held the little girls by their heels and spun them around while they squealed. He told stories. "My dad would be the Old Witch," recalled Diane, "and chase Sharon and me all over the house and we'd go into a little dark corner and yell 'The Old Witch is coming,' and we'd scream and hide our heads and love it."

"We weren't raised with the idea that this is a great man," said Sharon. "He was Daddy. He went to work every morning. He came home every night."

If there was any problem for the girls it was something entirely out of Walt's control. On March 1, 1932, Charles Lindbergh's baby son had been stolen from his bed. The aviator was one of the most admired men in America, and news of the kidnapping pushed the economy out of the headlines. A $50,000 ransom was paid to the kidnapper. After six weeks, the child's tiny corpse was found half-buried, five miles from his home.

This terrifying event had more than passing interest to Walt and Lilly. The Disneys put steel-reinforced screens on the nursery windows. They avoided public outings and halted publicity about their children. It was tempting to publish pictures of Diane and Sharon hugging Mickey Mouse, but Walt didn't permit it.

Walt and Lilly made efforts not to spoil their daughters. Although Walt's tendency was to heap endless mounds of toys and games on his children, he learned not to give them each little thing they desired immediately. "I think

Dad realized after a time, that the more you want things, the better you like them when you get them," Diane said.

Still, the Disney girls had no doubts at all about where they stood with Walt. "Daddy is a pushover," Diane summed up the relationship many years later. "He's the biggest softie in the world."

# Snow White

© Walt Disney Enterprises

*"Walt just kept progressing. He was the
first with sound. He was the first with
color. Then he wanted to make a feature.
I didn't want him to. I thought, 'We're
doing all right. Let's not go any
farther than this.' "*
—LILLIAN DISNEY

By 1934, Walt had a large house, played polo at a ritzy club, owned seven
polo ponies, and had a gardener. The resounding commercial success of the
past few years had brought him, and his family, a highly comfortable life.

Then Walt decided to risk it all—by plunging into debt to create the world's
first full-length cartoon feature. Shorts were only about six minutes; a feature
would be on the screen for twenty times that. Initial estimates, which turned
out to be wildly low, put the price for making a feature at upwards of half-a-
million dollars.

Roy and Lilly were distressed. The Disney brothers had finally figured out
how to make a living out of shorts. Why jeopardize everything now?

The possibility of total financial calamity appeared not to trouble Walt at
all. Success hadn't made him conservative or fearful about losing what he had
built. "People look at me and say 'The guy has no regard for money.' That is
not true. I have had regard for money," he explained. "There's some people
who worship money as something you've got to have piled up in a big pile
somewhere. I've only thought of money in one way—and that is to do something with."

In fact, Walt had good business reasons to develop a new market for his work. A new fad in the mid-1930s, the double feature, left less time for movie houses to show several cartoons. What's more, Walt had lost a great deal of the edge he had over other studios in cartoon shorts. All his competitors had sound. When Walt's exclusive rights to Technicolor expired, most had comparably good color as well. Other companies were even developing stars, like Popeye, with strong personalities.

"I knew if we wanted to get anywhere, we'd have to go beyond the short subject," Walt said. He thought about making feature-length cartoons out of *Rip Van Winkle* and *Alice in Wonderland*. Finally, he selected *Snow White*. "I had sympathetic dwarfs, you see? I had the heavy. I had the prince. And the girl. The romance. I thought it was a perfect story."

Walt's acting ability and intense enthusiasm combined to fire up his staff. One night in early 1934, he bought dinner for a group of artists, then led them to a barely lit stage. There, Walt acted out the whole story of Snow White single-handedly. He was the Evil Queen threatening Snow White. He was Snow White picking flowers. He was each of Seven Dwarfs. After three exhausting hours, he was the Prince kissing Snow White; then he was Snow White waking up.

His performance totally won over his audience. But outside the studio, industry gossips thought Walt had gone berserk. The arguments against a full-length cartoon were loud and numerous: "Nobody will sit still for an hour and a half of cartoons. . . . The colors will hurt their eyes. . . . People will just get tired of ninety minutes of gags. . . . How can you believe a cartoon girl and a cartoon boy falling in love?" *Snow White* was widely known as "Disney's Folly."

Walt ignored it all. A trip to Europe with Lilly, Edna, and Roy in 1935 only heightened his confidence. He discovered that European theaters were showing six Mickey cartoons in a row. Audiences were delighted and the optometrists' business increased not a bit.

Between 1934 and the end of 1937, the studio continued to expand. At the start of this period, Walt had a staff of nearly 200, including a full orchestra, forty animators, and forty-five assistant animators. In 1935, he added 300 more artists.

Though *Snow White* was his main focus, Walt continued to oversee the million-and-one details of the studio as well. One day while listening to the radio, for example, Walt discovered a man named Clarence Nash who was proficient at bird noises. He hired him immediately at $40 a week—double what he earned at his dairy company job. Nash spent a year at the studio doing odd sounds for cartoons, before his distinctive duck speech found its way to the mouth of a new Disney character, Donald Duck. The cantankerous duck soon joined Mickey and Goofy as one of Disney's top stars.

Walt touched each individual cartoon in some way. He even continued to provide the voice of Mickey Mouse. Half-jokingly, he said his greatest strength was that he did nothing *really* well, but knew something about everything—art, acting, music, mechanics, and story development. He had an uncanny ability to see how someone else's animation or story line or gag could be improved. "Lots of times we'd get mad," said Ward Kimball, one of Disney's star animators who joined the studio in 1934. "But then we'd say 'Why didn't I think of that?'

"If a story had a problem or we were at a dead end, he'd look at it and *boom*, he'd pull the solution out of left field."

In the three years that *Snow White* was in production, the studio produced sixty-four short cartoons, won five Academy Awards, produced the first color Mickey cartoon ("The Band Concert") and launched Donald's career. As if that didn't keep his employees busy enough, Walt also stepped up art training, expanding classes to two half-days each week as well as every night.

His artists studied motion—from raindrops falling in a breeze to giraffes craning their necks at the Los Angeles Zoo. Walt wrote, "I definitely feel that we cannot do the fantastic things based on the real unless we first know the real."

As two million frames of film were completed for *Snow White*, every aspect of the plot and music was thoroughly discussed. The dwarfs' names were hotly debated. Walt considered Shifty, Nifty, Woeful, Soulful, Flabby, Crabby, Awful, and Snoopy! Even after several months they were called Doc, Grumpy, Happy, Sleepy, Sneezy, Bashful, and Seventh. Finally, Walt decided on Dopey—though others in the studio feared that it would sound like the seventh dwarf was on drugs.

"Disney had only one rule," said an animator, "whatever we did had to be better than anybody else could do it." The invention of the multiplane camera allowed his animators to take their craft a full step forward. This device permitted them to create the illusion of depth by stacking several paintings on

81

glass. The scenery on the painting closest to the camera appeared closer than that on the painting below it. In late 1936 and early 1937, the new technique was used to create an award-winning *Silly Symphony* called "The Old Mill." "The Goddess of Spring," another *Silly Symphony*, gave artists a chance to experiment with the human form.

Even though artists worked nights and weekends on *Snow White* without additional pay, the bill added up fast. Walt's original $500,000 price tag had turned to $1 million and then to $1.5 million. Roy pleaded with the bankers to advance them more money. "We have considered changing the name of the picture from *Snow White* to *Frankenstein*," said Walt.

The three-minute sequence in which the dwarfs sing "Heigh-Ho" as they tramp through the woods took nearly six months to finish. One other complicated scene was completely animated and then cut, because it didn't help the plot.

When the film was nearly done, Walt decided that Snow White was too pale, and had his inkers and painters go back and add blush to her cheeks in

© Walt Disney Enterprises

*The opening of* Snow White and the Seven Dwarfs *with a star-studded premiere drew a huge crowd.*

tens of thousands of drawings. To Walt's dismay, he couldn't fix everything that bothered him, however. The film had to be out before Christmas, to catch the huge holiday moviegoing rush. So, although the prince jiggled unbecomingly in spots, there simply wasn't time to smooth out his shakes.

On December 21, 1937, *Snow White* opened in the Carthay Circle Theater in Los Angeles. It was one of the glitziest, showiest premieres in memory. Charlie Chaplin was there, as was Cary Grant, Jack Benny, Shirley Temple, Ginger Rogers, George Burns, and Gracie Allen.

Disney animator Ward Kimball remembered the night: "The highlight was at the climax of the film, when Snow White is presumed to be dead and she's laid out on the slab. . . . Here was a cartoon, and here was the audience crying. The biggest stars, you name them, were all wiping their eyes."

When the movie ended, the audience rose from their seats and cheered.

# Tragedy

© Walt Disney Enterprises

"I hope Dad will listen to reason and
stop doing the heavy work that he has been
doing. . . . I can't understand why he won't
take things easier and behave himself."
—WALT DISNEY
*Letter to Flora*

*Flora and
Elias Disney*

Less than two weeks after the sensational premiere of *Snow White*, a joyous Disney clan held a big fiftieth wedding anniversary party for Flora and Elias. Walt borrowed a studio tape recorder for the occasion. "This is station D-I-S-N-E-Y," announced Roy, "continuing with the broadcast of the golden wedding anniversary of Mr. and Mrs. Disney."

On the tape, Walt interviewed his parents in mock-newsman style, jokingly drawing them out on their early lives and feigning exasperation at his father's one-word answers. The Disney brothers teased their folks. Uncle Robert offered his congratulations on a long marriage. The family sang together—off-key; four-year-old Diane mispronounced the word "congratulations," and little Roy, then eight, read the story of Pinocchio.

There was obviously a great deal to celebrate for the family. All of the Disney children, except for Ray, were happily married. There were now five grand-children, and Flora and Elias had recently agreed to move to Hollywood, where Walt and Roy had bought them a small house.

For years, the Disney brothers had been concerned about their parents. Despite their sons' achievements, the elder Disneys insisted on living life much

84

as they always had. They ran a rooming house in Portland and continued to work hard despite failing health.

Flora scared everyone when she had a small stroke in the mid-thirties, and then several more in quick succession. "I think you should keep in mind that your health is worth far more than any money that might be derived by trying to do too much with your own hands," Walt wrote his mother. "After all, money is no good to us if we do not have the good health to enjoy it."

Now, finally, the aging couple had agreed to take it easy. Quickly, they settled into California life, enjoying their new house and the housekeeper Walt and Roy provided. Lilly and Edna helped them decorate.

With the exception of Ruth, who remained in Portland with her husband, Theodore Beecher, the Disney family was all together and as close as ever. Walt and Roy tried to talk Herb into entering their business, but he insisted that he liked being a mail carrier and a mail carrier he would stay. Walt often said that his oldest brother was the happiest Disney of them all, since he was so contented with his lot in life.

Ray sold insurance. He never married and was an odd character by everyone's estimation. He smoked cigars constantly and tooled down Los Angeles streets on an old-fashioned bicycle with a big basket in front. "Actually, he looked very much like the witch in *The Wizard of Oz* on that bike," one relative remarked.

© Walt Disney Enterprises

*The Disney brothers—Walt, Roy, Herbert, and Ray—were always close to their mother, Flora. She kept the family together even during hard times.*

On weekends, Walt often brought his two children to visit his parents and talk. On Sundays, the whole family continued to meet regularly at Roy's house to play vicious games of croquet. The older brothers often ganged up on Walt, who generally lost, and there was great suspicion that Ray moved the ball when no one was looking. Afterwards, they would all exchange small talk and sit around eating barbecued burgers and boiled corn. "It was very midwestern," said Roy Edward Disney.

Then in November, 1938, tragedy struck.

Flora had been complaining about the gas furnace in her new house for weeks, and Walt had sent a studio handyman to fix it. The repair wasn't adequate. Early on the morning of November 26, 1938, poisonous fumes began spreading slowly through their home.

Alma, the couple's housekeeper, was downstairs fixing oatmeal for breakfast. Flora got up, leaving Elias in bed, and walked into the bathroom. As she washed, she grew dizzy and then fainted, overcome by the gas. Elias found her on the floor. He tried to carry her out, but he, too, succumbed to the fumes and fell unconscious into the hall.

Downstairs, Alma realized that she was rather woozy. She rushed upstairs to see if the Disneys were all right, and found Elias lying in the hall.

Unable to get the windows open or to move the couple, Alma ran for help from the man next door. Together, they dragged Flora and Elias out of the house. It was too late for Flora.

Elias never really recovered. Whether it was the gas he had inhaled, or the loss of Flora, for the last few years of his life he was a shell of the man he had once been.

Nearly twenty years later, Sharon was driving Walt to the studio one day, and as they were cruising down Sunset Boulevard, the conversation turned to Walt's parents. "Where are they buried, Daddy?" asked Sharon.

"They're in Forest Lawn," he answered. "I don't want to talk about it." Sharon saw his eyes well up.

Two decades after the tragic accident, Walt cried when he thought about that day in 1938. Nothing more was said.

# The Boss

"I used to get mad and blow my top—
kind of a Donald-Duck-type thing."
—WALT DISNEY

© Walt Disney Enterprises

Little was ever mentioned at Walt Disney Productions about Walt and Roy's family tragedy. They were devastated by their mother's death, but let few see. Work continued at a frantic pace.

By the end of 1938, the studio was working on three more feature films: *Pinocchio*, the story of a wooden marionette who wants to become a little boy; *Fantasia*, in which Walt wanted to create a new sort of entertainment, mixing animation and music; and *Bambi*, the story of a young deer and his adventures.

Theater owners clamored for more dwarfs in the package. But Walt insisted that Grumpy, Sneezy, and the gang were going into permanent retirement. "One thing I've never believed in is sequels," said Walt. "It goes back to when they wanted me to do more pigs. I reluctantly made more pigs. When they wanted me to make more dwarfs, I said no."

Each of the three features represented possible roads for the future of cartoons. *Bambi* was an exercise in believability. Animals would talk, but be drawn as realistically as possible. No gloves on the mice or sailor hats on the ducks. Deer and rabbits were kept on the studio lot so artists could study their movements.

© Walt Disney Enterprises

*"We cannot do the fantastic things . . . unless we first know the real,"* Walt wrote. He had his artists diligently study deer and other animal life for Bambi.

*Fantasia*, initially dubbed "The Concert Feature," was a test of creative imagination. The feature had started as a Mickey Mouse cartoon telling the story of the Sorcerer's Apprentice. But it soon moved into uncharted territory. With the brilliant conductor Leopold Stokowski adapting famous pieces of classical music, Walt's animators were challenged to imagine how to draw what they heard. They visualized Beethoven's Sixth Symphony as a story about the Greek gods; Igor Stravinsky's *Rite of Spring* was the birth of the earth and the age of the dinosaurs; Amilcare Ponchielli's *Dance of the Hours* was an animal ballet complete with impossibly dainty hippos in tutus.

*Pinocchio* didn't break new ground. Like *Snow White*, it was a good old-fashioned fairy tale. But Walt wanted to give his staff a chance to use all they had learned on *Snow White* to make this film a technical masterpiece. Backgrounds were far more elaborate. Artists were sent to sketch seascapes on the Pacific coast. Models of clocks and toys from Geppetto's shop were built, so that animators could carefully study the movements before drawing them.

Walt set about building a new studio in Burbank, California. When completed, at a cost of $3 million, it would be the envy of Hollywood. Volleyball and badminton courts . . . a gym on the roof of the building . . . a full-service restaurant with a snack shop and soda fountain that delivered to employees' offices . . . beautifully kept grounds with park benches . . . offices which all had outside views and most of which had the north light that artists crave.

Most important, the buildings were air-conditioned. In the old studio, the room in which cartoons were screened had been called the "sweatbox," because it was so often intolerably hot. The new studio would be cool all through the humid summer. The screening rooms continued to be called sweatboxes, though. Walt made artists sweat when their work was being reviewed, regardless of the temperature.

Some Disney employees, watching all this money going into the new studio, grumbled that they hadn't been fairly paid for all their work on *Snow White*. News that *Snow White* had taken in $8 million made them think Walt was using $100 bills to light his cigarettes.

In fact, personal wealth meant as little as ever to Walt. He wanted to use his profits to take animation into a golden age. The Disney company was the only one that could do it; other studios had failed with their efforts at feature-length animated films.

Walt's single-minded devotion to his work translated into anger when he was displeased with someone's work. "I'd just tear the hell out of them," he admitted. "I just sometimes feel like a dirty heel, the way I pound, pound, pound." The sound of Walt's cough—a warning that he was approaching—could tie an employee's stomach up in knots. When he let loose with a burst of furious words, Walt seemed oblivious to whom he hurt. He would scathe people who had worked with him for years as easily as those who had been with him for days. Walt left more than one grown man in tears.

Even some of Walt's most trusted and well-liked employees resented his volatile temperament. Ward Kimball was an animator and director who started at the studio in 1934, when he was twenty. He called Walt "one of our American homemade geniuses," and was awed by the constant outpouring of ideas from Walt's mind. Still, "if there was one thing I was critical of," said Kimball, "it's that he jumped on people in front of others. . . . In story meetings he was very harsh on people who brought up an idea that he felt didn't fit into a discussion. As a result, people would hold back because they didn't want to be bawled out or yelled at. But that was Walt's way of creating."

Still in his mid-thirties, Walt was monarch over a kingdom of his own

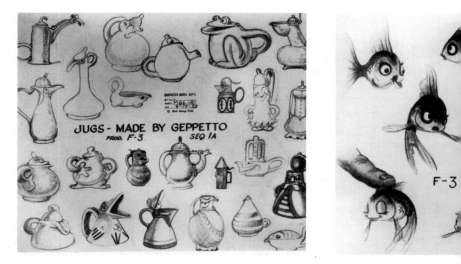

*Before animation of features such as* Pinocchio *began, artists made hundreds of sketches of props and characters.*

creation. He loathed laziness and dishonesty. He didn't like to hear anything negative. He had an aversion to dirty jokes, office gossip, and snobbism. A childhood dislike of "snitches" stayed with him, and employees who had a problem with a superior or subordinate were unlikely to get satisfaction by complaining to him.

This created problems, since Walt's choices for middle-management positions were sometimes questionable. Artists and writers frequently complained that their immediate bosses were less talented individuals who imitated Walt's demanding style, but had none of his imagination, charm, enthusiasm, or energy.

At the same time, Walt could be thoughtful and considerate. Employees marvelled at his ability to ask about their wives and children by name. A baby's birth was greeted with huge bouquets of flowers. When a young artist was out of work for nearly half a year because of illness, Walt unquestioningly sent his salary check home week after week.

He firmly believed in lifetime learning and constantly stimulated his staff with educational experiences. When one employee mentioned that he was taking a class in film drama at the University of Southern California, Walt asked him to arrange for the class to be taught at the studio. He invited a series

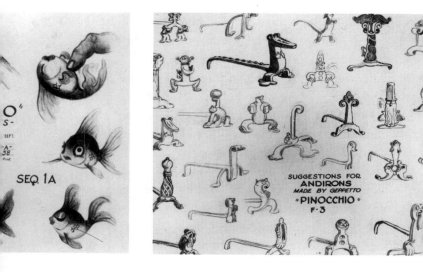

SUGGESTIONS FOR
ANDIRONS
MADE BY GEPPETTO
• PINOCCHIO •
F-3

SEQ. 1A

of famous men—like Alexander Woollcott, Aldous Huxley, and Frank Lloyd Wright—to lecture at the studio or show their work.

John Hench, a Disney artist, writer, and ideas-man, first joined the studio during the production of *Fantasia*. He loved classical music and the concept of the film, but disliked ballet. When Walt asked him to work on a ballet sequence, he asked for another assignment.

"What do you know about ballet?" Walt asked.

"I don't know anything about it."

"Well, here's what you're going to do. You're going to find out something about it."

Walt immediately arranged for his employee to get season tickets to the famous Ballet Russe of Monte Carlo and spend time with the dancers backstage. The young man discovered that he loved ballet. "It really made a difference. I made friends and it changed my life," he said.

"Walt was a personality who seemed to be all over everywhere and had great curiosity. He was very excited about what he was doing. And he lived and breathed it and finally it rubbed off on you."

Partially in response to Walt's pressures—and partially because they were an awfully creative bunch to begin with—the studio took on an almost hys-

91

terical air. Walt didn't join in on the high jinks, but he was tolerant of them. As long as good work was being turned out, he would put up with almost anything.

A great deal of liquor was consumed; Walt would turn his head and try to ignore the somewhat-too-happy hellos he got when he walked out of the studio. Football games in the corridors were common, as was office croquet with teeny-tiny wickets. Dirty movies were occasionally shown—the senior staff was still primarily male. Practical jokes were the order of the day.

On one occasion, Walt Kelly—a Disney animator who went on to create the comic strip "Pogo"—targeted a fellow animator who took great pride in successfully throwing his coat across the room onto a coatrack. Kelly sawed the coat rack into dozens of small pieces and taped it back together so the breaks wouldn't show. When the victim came back from drinking lunch he tossed his coat, as usual, and nearly passed out when the whole rack came tumbling apart like a house of cards.

Even public safety wasn't considered when it was time to have a little fun. Bob Moore was a longtime Disney artist. He recalled one episode, shortly after he joined the studio in early 1940: "Our offices were all in a row, connected by a series of doors," he said, "and I was in the very last office in the row. So one day another artist, Freddy Moore, came into my room while I was working. I heard this hammering and I turned around to see him putting up a small target on my far wall. I didn't think anything of it.

"Then, pretty soon, I hear this thud. There's an arrow sticking in the target. He and another animator were shooting a bow and arrow through all these doorways into the target. Somebody could have been killed.

"You had to have a white flag on a stick if you wanted to get out of your room."

# Strike!

"To me, the entire situation is a
catastrophe. The spirit that played such an
important part in the building of the
cartoon medium has been destroyed."
—WALT DISNEY
Letter to newspaper columnist
Westbrook Pegler

© Walt Disney Enterprises

Walt was plowing every nickel from *Snow White* back into *Pinocchio*, *Fantasia*, and *Bambi*. Then in September, 1939, when Nazi Germany invaded Poland, and World War II began for the European nations, foreign markets were cut off and nearly half the studio's income disappeared. It could hardly have happened at a worse time.

Expenses for *Fantasia* had mounted as Walt experimented with new sound systems. Intense dedication to artistic detail meant *Bambi* was taking much longer than expected. *Pinocchio*, too, was behind schedule and way over budget. After the first six months of work, Walt had halted production, complaining that the puppet was unappealing and bratty. Animators and writers struggled with the problem until Walt suggested adding a cricket/narrator who could serve as Pinocchio's conscience. "We finally ended up with a little man with no ears," said animator Ward Kimball about Jiminy Cricket. "That was the only thing about him that was like an insect."

Despite all the work, and critical raves, *Pinocchio* failed to recover its $2.6 million cost when it came out in 1940. The absence of the foreign markets, and a gloomy national mood, combined to hurt the picture at the box office.

*Fantasia* had even bigger problems. The U.S. government decided that the materials needed for *Fantasia's* special sound system could be better used for the national defense. Walt had to show the movie with ordinary equipment in most theaters.

Worse yet, many moviegoers resented being told what they were supposed to picture when listening to music. A critic in the *New York Herald-Tribune* seemed to say that *Fantasia* would lead to the collapse of civilization. Some people stayed away because they thought any movie with classical music was just too uppity for them.

The final blow came when RKO—the distributor he was now using instead of United Artists—forced Walt to cut his masterpiece from two hours to 82 minutes, so that it could be part of a double feature. Walt refused to do the editing himself. As far as he was concerned, it was like giving the Mona Lisa a haircut.

One afternoon, after it became clear how bad things were, Roy called Walt into his office with a worried look on his face. He explained to Walt that the studio was teetering on the brink. It had 1,500 people on the payroll. Many employees were demanding raises. *Snow White* profits were long gone. The studio had $4.5 million of debt, with no way to pay it.

Walt started to laugh.

"What are you laughing at?"

"I was just thinking back," Walt said, "to when we couldn't borrow a thousand dollars."

Roy started to grin, too.

Walt and Roy talked about old times for a while. Finally, they decided that the bankers were the ones who should really be worrying. "Gee, what are they going to do?" Walt asked, chortling.

Though the two brothers reassured each other, financially strapped workers were frightened.

Rumors spread: "He's going to lay us off. . . . He's hiring women to work cheaper. . . . He's making a fortune off our work. . . . He's going to cut our pay. . . ."

Walt didn't want to lay anyone off. "I hated to fire anybody," he said. "I'd think, gee, he's got five kids. . . ."

Instead, he decided to sell stock in the company. Henry Ford, the automobile-company founder, warned him that he would regret the day he let investors in. But there didn't seem to be a choice.

Stock was sold at $25 a share and brought in enough money to keep the company going. In order to reward loyal employees, the Disneys gave them one-fifth of all the stock issued. Many people think that employee stock plans—which allow workers to share ownership of the company—were first created in the 1970s. Walt and Roy were doing it in 1940.

Shortly after the stock was issued, its price started to fall. It went to twenty. Then eighteen. Then ten. It ended up at three. All along the way, Walt used what little cash he had to buy more.

His employees didn't have similar confidence. They sold shares as the stock's price went down. Walt had assumed the price of the stock wouldn't matter to them; that they'd want to remain part-owners of the company they worked for. He was wrong. Faith is terrific—but when the rent is due, money in the bank can look better.

Though Walt's senior animators were the best paid in the industry, many younger staffers got barely enough to live on. A bonus system which rewarded the best workers made many suspicious that they were being paid less than they deserved. Their resentment grew when they saw all the money that went into the new studio.

With 1,500 or more employees diluting direct loyalty to Walt, inevitably talk of unionization began to flare up among his artists. Hollywood—and the rest of the United States, for that matter—had been a hotbed of labor-movement activity ever since 1933 when Franklin D. Roosevelt signed a law that forced companies to allow unions to organize. Most of the nonartistic members of the Disney crew already had joined unions by 1941, without much of a battle on either side. Only the artists, who made up about half the Disneys' staff, were still not members.

The Screen Cartoonists Guild was particularly anxious to unionize the Disney shop. The Guild saw the animation industry as a series of dominoes. Disney was the first in line. If its artists could be unionized, the rest of the industry would fall as well.

Walt grew angry at what he thought was disloyalty on the part of those who wanted to join a union, and threw up a wall of silence on the subject. He saw the strikers—particularly the leaders—as deserters. All through the events that led up to the big strike in May, 1941, Walt's mistake was in expecting employees to act like relatives. It was the same error Walt had been making all his professional life; he so loved the idea of a big, happy family that he kept trying to find one in his studio.

Had Walt gone directly to his union-oriented employees to work things out, he might well have been able to control the situation. Instead, the studio's lawyer, Gunther Lessing, did most of the talking for him. "Gunny," as Walt called him, had been with the studio for years and was a poor choice to smooth ruffled feathers. He was a man inclined to answer questions by rolling his eyes to show how stupid he thought the questioner was. Lessing tried to persuade the artists that they didn't need an outside union, but that they'd be better off with an in-house Disney union.

For months the struggle simmered. When Walt finally offered to allow a vote—to see if the majority of his workers really wanted the Screen Cartoonists Guild or not, Herbert Sorrell, a well known union organizer, turned him down flat. "I don't go for that vote stuff," he said. "You sign with me or I'll strike you."

"I've got to have a vote," said Walt. "I'm not signing with you on your say-so."

"All right. I warned you. I can make a dust bowl out of your place here."

On February 10, 1941, Walt finally decided to talk directly to the staff. For three hours he tried his hardest to reach out and explain himself to his employees. He talked about the days when he couldn't afford to eat or pay the rent. . . . He explained that in the middle of the Depression other cartoon-makers had cut salaries by as much as fifty percent while he had refused to do so. . . . He boasted that he had given nearly half-a-million dollars in bonuses to his employees in the previous seven years.

It was too late. People had already made their decisions. Those who wanted the union thought the speech was insincere.

In April, Roy announced that the loss of the foreign markets meant there were going to have to be salary cuts and layoffs. The higher-ranking workers—including Walt and Roy—would take the biggest cuts. The union insisted this was just a ploy to scare the workers.

On May 27, Art Babbitt, one of Disney's best animators and one of the leaders of the union, was fired. The union felt that this was because of his union activity.

The next day nearly half of the Disney artists went out on strike. A number

© Walt Disney Enterprises

*With the strike in full flower, Roy took drastic steps, including shutting down the plant.*

NOTICE TO ALL EMPLOYEES

The Board of Directors of Walt Disney Productions has today found it necessary to order the temporary suspension of general operations of its plant until September 2, 1941 commencing as of the close of business today and to lay off all personnel without pay excepting those necessary to perform essential maintenance work and the completion of certain emergency commitments. Employees necessary for such services have been separately notified.

All employees are requested to appear for work on September 2, 1941 unless previously notified by mail of a different date. All employees working through tonight will be paid up to Monday night (August 18th). Checks for pay to Monday night may be picked up at the Buena Vista gate at 3:30 P. M. Monday. Checks not picked up by 5:30 P. M. will be mailed to the employees Monday night.

The management will not be responsible for any personal effects left in the studio during the time the operations are suspended.

August 15, 1941      By order of the Board of Directors of WALT DISNEY PRODUCTIONS

of other, nonstriking employees refused to cross their picket lines. Walt was sure it would be over in a few days. But as the days turned to weeks, the battle turned vicious.

Strike headquarters were set up across the street from the studio. There the strikers picketed, chanted, and taunted Walt at every opportunity. They called him a "rat . . . a yellow-dog employer . . . an exploiter of labor." What hurt the most were accusations that he was rolling in wealth. "The fact is," he wrote, "every damn thing I have is tied up in this business."

By August, Walt was absolutely sick over the whole affair. He had become convinced that the forces running the union were sinister ones—Communists. Even Walt's daughters were caught up in the anger of the fray. Four-year-old Sharon had proclaimed in a serious voice, "Pickets is bad people." Thereafter when Diane and her little sister were driven past the studio they would yell Sharon's comment loudly out the window of the car.

A trip to South America in the fall was a godsend for Walt. The State Department had asked him to take a twelve-week tour to help improve relations with South American countries and gather information for upcoming cartoons and possible features. A select group of artists and writers accompanied Walt and Lilly, including her sister Hazel and Hazel's new husband, Disney employee Bill Cottrell.

Just before he left, Walt poured out his heart in a letter to newspaper columnist Westbrook Pegler. "I am not licked," he wrote, "I am incensed. . . . The lies, the twisted half-truths that were placed in the public prints cannot be easily forgotten. . . . The thing that worries me is that people only read headlines and never take enough time to follow through and find out the truth. . . . This expedition . . . gives me a chance to get away from this god-awful nightmare."

During the course of the trip, Walt got word that Elias had died. Though Walt was saddened, he accepted the news calmly. In the years since Flora's death, Elias had acted as though he was simply waiting to join her.

By the time Walt and Lilly got back to the Burbank studio the strike had been settled. Walt was not happy with the terms, which gave the strikers everything they wanted including a guarantee that in any future layoffs, strikers and nonstrikers would be fired in equal numbers. Subsequently, a number of the gifted artists who had struck left on their own—they no longer found the Disney studio an enjoyable place to work.

"It was the toughest period I've had in my whole life," Walt said. His relationship with his employees changed forever. He began to look at them in a more cynical way. No longer would he keep people on the payroll because he didn't have the heart to fire them. Staffers had to punch into a time clock now. The snack shop that delivered to offices was closed.

Gone were the days when he thought of the whole studio crew as a family. Family didn't hurt you like that.

# Nutziland

© Walt Disney Enterprises

*"I was the only studio in town that was practically a war plant."*
—WALT DISNEY

Surprisingly, one of Disney's best films was completed during the strike. Released on Halloween Day, 1941, *Dumbo*, the story of a flying elephant, was an overnight hit. Only 64 minutes long, it had memorable music, a powerful plot, and superb animation. By Thanksgiving, songs from the film were on every radio station, and *Time* magazine was planning to put the large-eared movie star on the cover of its Christmas issue.

That particular cover never appeared.

On December 7, 1941, the Japanese air force bombed the American naval base at Pearl Harbor, Hawaii. In the worst military disaster in American history, nearly three thousand men were killed.

In one violent stroke, the Japanese destroyed the comforting notion that the United States was beyond attack. On the West Coast, panic spread; would California be next?

That night—war would be declared the next day—Walt got a call from a studio manager. "Walt," he said, voice shaking, "the Army is moving in on us. I said I'd have to call you. And they said 'Call him. But we're moving in anyway.' "

Before hours had passed, seven hundred soldiers had taken over the Disney studio. They were there to help protect the nearby Lockheed aircraft plant from enemy attack. Guards were posted at the gates. Security checks were run to make sure there were no spies on the Disney staff. The restaurant was turned into a mess hall. Three million rounds of ammunition were stored on the studio parking lot. For the next eight months, these soldiers lived in the studio as artists doubled up in offices to make space.

When the war began, the Disneys dropped work on future projects like *Alice in Wonderland* and *Peter Pan*. Only *Bambi* was completed. The cost to the studio was enormous, but Walt saw no other choice. The studio plunged into the war effort, producing training films like "Aircraft Carrier Landing Signals," "Basic Map-Reading," and the unforgettable "Ward Care of Psychotic Patients."

Even though the studio was near the brink of financial disaster, Walt wanted to donate his services in making these films. The government refused. They insisted Walt take a profit. Then, because the military men had no idea how much went into making a cartoon, they spent the rest of the war arguing about Walt's bills.

Donald Duck, Goofy, the Seven Dwarfs, and other Disney characters were drafted. They became the stars of a number of shorts designed to educate or inspire the public. The most famous of these was "Der Fuehrer's Face," which won the Academy Award in 1943. It featured Donald Duck in a dream about life in Nazi Germany—called "Nutziland" in the cartoon. The Duck has an impossible, grueling job in a factory there and virtually nothing to eat. His breakfast is sawdust accompanied by a cup of coffee he has made by quickly dunking one coffee bean into a cup. He winds up throwing tomatoes at a picture of Hitler. This short was translated into a number of languages and smuggled into Europe, where it provided much-needed laughter for men and women who were trying to stop the advance of the Germans.

Everything considered, the studio output was ten times larger than it had been before the war. Much of the material was inferior to the usual Disney product but it was still an enormous strain for everyone involved. Under this kind of pressure, Walt was infuriated by the government officials with whom he had to work.

One maddening argument centered on a Donald Duck cartoon made to persuade people to pay their taxes. The troubles began when Walt showed the half-finished cartoon to Secretary of the Treasury Henry Morgenthau, who questioned Walt's casting. "I'd always visualized you creating a little character here that would be Mr. Taxpayer," said Morgenthau.

Then his assistant piped up. "I don't like Donald Duck."

Walt's eyebrow arched. "Maybe you don't," he said, trying to control his rage, "but there's an awful lot of people who do."

Then, to the Secretary of the Treasury: "I've given you Donald Duck. That's the equivalent of giving you Clark Gable out of the MGM stable. . . . He'll open the doors to the theaters."

After the cartoon was completed, Walt was accused by a congressman of trying to profit unfairly from the war. His costs had been high because the Treasury Department had wanted the cartoon done very quickly. But he hadn't tried to make a penny of excess profit. In fact, he had lost a great deal of money when theaters cancelled their regular orders for Donald Duck cartoons in order to show this one—which they got for free. "Here we broke our necks and then I got postcards calling me unpatriotic," moaned Walt.

Walt jumped at the chance to make a film without government funding or interference. He had been fascinated by a new book, *Victory Through Air Power* by Major Alexander DeSeversky, which argued for greater use of aircraft instead of battleships in fighting the war. Walt was convinced this was an important idea, and could help win the war. So, he turned it into a film, part live action, part animation.

It just about broke even. But it may have had some influence where influence counted.

British Prime Minister Winston Churchill was impressed by the film. He insisted that President Roosevelt watch it, too.

When the D-Day invasion—the beginning of the end for the Nazis—used an enormous amount of air support, there were some who felt that a note of thanks should have gone to Walt Disney.

# The Family Man

*"There were two Walts. At the studio he was a man with a mission in life. He couldn't allow sentiment to interfere. That's the Walt most people knew. They didn't know the family man."*

—HERB RYMAN
Artist and family friend

© Walt Disney Enterprises

*Sharon and Diane with their father*

Through the years, Walt's employees spent so much time trying to figure him out that their husbands and wives grew sick of the topic. At parties, on vacations, at intimate dinners, the conversation would inevitably turn to discussions of what made him tick.

But there was one part of Walt's life that was a closed book to most people at the studio. Walt and his family doggedly guarded their privacy. This protectiveness, combined with Walt's passion for work, led some at the studio to assume that his family life was unimportant and neglected. Or that the sometimes-difficult boss was a difficult husband and father.

A far different portrait comes from those who knew Walt best—his few good friends, nieces, daughters, and wife. They paint a picture of a highly sentimental man who was devoted to his family. If Walt assumed the characteristics of Elias on the job, at home he was often more like Flora—a playmate for the children, with a silly sense of humor, a kind disposition, and encouraging manner.

At work, Walt was unquestionably in charge. At home, Lilly ruled the roost. At work, he seemed uncomfortable with physical contact. With Lilly and the girls, he was open and affectionate—always holding their hands or draping an arm around their shoulders. "I don't think he ever came home without kissing and hugging Aunt Lilly," Marjorie remembered.

At work, people worried about keeping him happy. When he was with Lilly, his concern was for her. At a hotel, he saw to it that she had her pick of the rooms. On a plane, she always got the window seat. Birthdays and anniversaries brought inscribed pieces of jewelry. On Valentine's Day one year, he reacted to her criticism of one of his hats by having it bronzed in the shape of a heart and filling it with orchids.

At work, he was a demanding perfectionist, who was sparing of praise. At home, he was ready to applaud each small success. "He would collect all my drawings and make me think I was wonderful," said Diane.

"If I was in a play, no matter how bad I was, he'd say, 'You did a great job, kid,' " recalled Sharon.

Staff expected him to have little patience for small talk or inefficiency. With the girls, he acted as though time had been created for relaxing and fun. Almost every weekend during the war years, Walt took his daughters to a zoo, an amusement area, or a neighborhood park.

"There was a brass ring on the merry-go-round at Griffith Park," recalled Sharon, "and you'd lean out as far as you could. If you got the brass ring you got a free ride." One day, Diane magically was able to grab the ring over and over again. "I suspected something was wrong," she said. "I found out later that Dad had bribed the kid who ran the ride to let me get it."

Walt rented, then purchased, a house in a resort community called Smoke Tree, a four-hour drive from Los Angeles in Palm Springs, California. Three times a year—at Easter, Christmas, and Thanksgiving—the Disneys would spend a relaxing week or so without telephones to disturb them. There, from the time the girls were quite young, he helped them learn how to ride horses. He always wore his cowboy hat and boots for the occasion.

On weekdays, their contact with Walt was obviously much less. Every hour Walt spent tinkering at the studio was one less he could spend with his family. Still, Walt drove the girls to school every day, and every night they waited until his arrival for dinner. "When is Daddy coming home? When is Daddy coming home?" the girls asked Lilly. These late evening meals could be fascinating or trying, depending on what had happened at the office and Walt's mood. "If you got into an argument it could be awful," said Diane. "But it could be fun and stimulating if he was excited about something he was doing."

Neither she nor Sharon remember their parents having serious arguments in front of them, although they certainly had their share of disagreements. They could never see eye to eye, for example, about animals. Walt was passionate about the subject. He yearned to raise dogs, but Lilly wouldn't hear about it. On one occasion he briefly reduced Lilly to tears when he insisted on bringing a baby goat home to live with them. "They're cute pets," he insisted—but finally gave in to Lilly. In a running battle with his family, he became the chief protector of all squirrels, and assorted vermin, on the Disney property. When the gardener complained that small animals were eating up all the fruit from the trees, Walt's answer was, "Plant more. Plant enough for everybody."

As the girls grew older, they discovered their father had great respect for their intellects. Though he and Lilly were Protestants, Walt permitted the girls to make their own decisions about religion. Diane went to a Catholic school and plunged into the rituals with enthusiasm. She even talked about becoming a nun. Eventually, however, Walt feared that Diane's education was a bit too narrowly focused, and he transferred her to another school.

After the war drew to a close and Diane got into her early teens, she was less infatuated with her daddy as a playmate. She became impatient on trips to the studio with him. Merry-go-rounds and zoos seemed like kiddie stuff.

But Sharon, who was only ten in 1947, hadn't lost interest at all. She became Walt's number-one pal, following him around wherever he went. Their house sat on a hill and the Disney property ran to the bottom. When Walt decided it would be fun to build a path through the overgrown shrubbery in the canyon, Sharon happily ran back and forth to the house to bring him soft drinks.

There were few hard rules and fewer chores. One of the only absolute restrictions was against lying. "I remember the only time I ever got spanked in my life," said Sharon. "Daddy had scolded me for something and I went up to my Aunt Grace's room and told her that Daddy had hit me. He hadn't. And he heard me say it. He whacked me across my bottom with his hand. He just would not accept dishonesty."

# The Perils of Walt

© Walt Disney Enterprises

"It seemed like a kind of hopeless thing to begin to pick up again."
—WALT DISNEY

*Long John Silver from* Treasure Island

Walt's life was a lot like the *Perils of Pauline* movies popular when he was a teenager. Every Pauline adventure ended with the heroine in life-threatening trouble: tied to a railroad track or hanging from a cliff. Naturally, she always wound up being rescued just in the nick of time—otherwise it would have been the end of the series.

The Second World War ended with Walt dangling from the cliff once again. *Bambi*, which was released in 1942, had done well, as had his films from South America. But the loss of the overseas market, the strike, and five full years doing primarily war-related cartoons had sapped the studio's energy. In the meantime, the cartoon shorts had lost their edge. After winning the first eight Academy Awards given for animated shorts, the Disney studio hadn't won one since 1942.

Although they were still deeply in debt, Walt was determined to plunge ahead with new projects. Roy wanted to move more slowly. He was the one who had to face nervous bankers and angry stockholders, after all. Walt avoided all such unpleasant meetings.

The Disney brothers had some violent fights over the future of their company—"screamers," Walt called them. "You're letting this place drive you nuts," Roy told Walt, "and that's one place I'm not going with you."

The studio floundered. "The company was about two inches from going under," remembered his son, Roy Edward.

Nothing seemed to go right. The Disneys' big hope for the immediate future was *Song of the South*, which was based on the famous Uncle Remus stories about Brer Rabbit and Brer Fox. Apart from the old Alice cartoons, and a short bit in a cartoon called *The Three Caballeros*, it was the studio's first attempt to combine cartoons with real actors and settings. Animators at the studio were delighted by the picture, which was the only major feature in development during the final years of the war. But when it was released in 1946, critics were disappointed.

Many found the plot confusing; the acting stilted except for James Baskett's Uncle Remus. They had grown to expect innovation and creativity from Disney features, and lambasted the studio for producing live-action footage no better, or different, than that of other studios.

Worse, the film was criticized in some quarters for being racist. Although Uncle Remus was the hero of the story, the National Urban League complained that *Song of the South* was "another . . . casting of the Negro in the servant role, depicting him as indolent, one who handles the truth lightly."

Walt, who liked the film very much, was stunned by this criticism. He had seen nothing negative in the story. But society was changing, and he had missed the boat. (Interestingly, in later showings, *Song of the South* was well received, though it continued to generate some controversy.)

In the meantime, Roy and Walt were battling over their next step. The compromise they hit on satisfied no one—a series of weakly plotted films that were little more than packages of short pieces. Fans were disappointed and critics became increasingly nasty. They accused Walt of "coasting," which was true. They called the films "grab bags," which was also true.

The magic of the Disney name was wearing a bit thin. "Let's do anything to get some action," Walt said.

The answer, he and Roy decided, was to diversify. Short cartoons were no longer a challenge and animated features were fearfully expensive. They needed other projects. "I wanted it set up so that all my eggs were not in that cartoon basket," Walt said.

Mentally freed from the restrictions of his old craft, Walt quickly found himself pioneering once again. Mystifying his staff, he commissioned a hus-band-and-wife team of filmmakers to take movies of Alaska. Everyone was baffled by the endless footage of wildlife, Eskimoes, forests, and glaciers that they sent in. Walt himself didn't know quite what to do with the miles of snowy film. But after a trip to Alaska with Sharon, he decided to turn it into a film about seals.

There were still plenty of skeptics. John Hench recalled: "You never saw anything so dull in your life as these seals . . . seals scratching their sides and their fannies and sniffing and looking at each other. And all seals look alike anyway. . . . But he was delighted with it."

Walt saw an opportunity that John Hench and everyone else missed. He knew instinctively that people loved to watch the antics of animals. All the creatures needed was a good story. With clever film editing, humorous writing, and the appropriate music, he could turn his seals into barking actors. He had the female seals arrive on the island to the tune of "Here Comes the Bride." When one of the male seals is basking on a rock, the narrator asks, "What more could one wish? A good home, adoring wives. A peaceful paradise." In

*Disney employees said that sniffing, snorting, cavorting seals were as boring as mud. But Walt thought other-wise when he made his first "True-Life Adventure."*

© Walt Disney Enterprises

years to come, this sugar-coated approach to nature films would come in for some ribbing. But at the time, the very concept of making a documentary film about animals for a general audience was revolutionary.

In fact, Walt had a tough time convincing his distributor, RKO, that anyone would pay to watch a bunch of seals. Back to the old Harry Reichenbach trick. Walt arranged to have the 27-minute film shown in the Crown Theater in Pasadena, California. That meant it qualified for an Academy Award. To absolutely no one's surprise, *Seal Island* won the award. After that, RKO gave Walt the go-ahead—and the True-Life Adventure Films were started.

At about the same time, Walt plunged into live-action films. The idea had appealed to him for years. They were cheaper and faster than cartoons and would lessen the studio's reliance on one big animated feature each year.

Once again, his distributors at RKO were discouraging. When he tried to make a live-action film called *So Dear To My Heart* they insisted he add cartoon footage. But when Walt embarked on *Treasure Island* in 1948, he wasn't going to let anyone push him around. The Robert Louis Stevenson book seemed perfect for the Disney audience: a time-tested story, plenty of adventure, comedy, and lots and lots of pirates.

Meanwhile, Walt still had a cartoon studio to run. With hundreds of animators and other artists on the payroll, he convinced Roy that it only was good common sense for the studio to embark on some new animated features. He made Roy happy by cutting expenses to the bone and encouraging employees to save money wherever they could. Then he started employees working on not one but *three* animated projects: *Alice in Wonderland* and *Peter Pan*, which had both been in the planning stage before the war, and *Cinderella*, a fairy tale in the nature of *Snow White*.

*Cinderella* was the first one in line. Walt and his story men zealously hammered out the plot. Then Walt put his most talented animators on it, including all of the "nine old men," the animators who formed the core of his team.

With the feature in good hands, the True-Life Adventures a solid success and the live-action pictures opening a whole world of new opportunities, Walt was ready to relax a little bit.

For nearly forty years, ever since he was a boy, he had worked at a merciless pace.

Now, it was time to play.

# The Man-Child

"*My brother was a kid all his life.*"
—RUTH DISNEY BEECHER

© Walt Disney Enterprises

At age 46, Walt was one of the most powerful men in Hollywood. Other Hollywood kings pleasured themselves with enormous mansions, teams of servants, and parties every night. They thought Walt was an odd duck. He avoided parties and showed no interest in starlets. He could easily afford caviar, but enjoyed chili and hamburgers more. To relax, he took Lilly on drives to the railroad tracks and waited for trains to chug by. "After they passed," she recalled, "he'd look at the vibrations in the tracks."

Walt's greatest pleasure was in seeing new things and talking to interesting people. Whether he was chatting with a scientist or a street sweeper, he asked question after probing question until he had some idea how they did their jobs. "He was a sponge, a human sponge," said Walt's niece, Marjorie.

Walt's personal passion for information was often surprising to people who knew he had never made it past his freshman year in high school. Although his grammar and pronunciation were often bad, and he relied on his secretary to correct his spelling, many people remarked that Walt was one of the most educated men they had met.

Now that he was famous he could indulge his desire to see everything up close. In planes, word would reach the pilot that Walt Disney wanted to visit the cockpit. Naturally, the answer was always an excited yes. When he visited New York on one occasion, he announced that he wanted to see the backstage operation of Radio City Music Hall, and spent hours with his brother-in-law and longtime associate Bill Cottrell examining all the pulleys, ropes, and hydraulic elevators that made the stage magic work. "It was a marvelous experience," recalled Cottrell. "You didn't have the opportunity very often to see those kinds of things."

In the summer of 1948, he took his first nonwork trip in years to the Chicago Train Fair. This festival featured over thirty old-time locomotives and trains, dozens of exhibits, and a spectacular show called "Wheels-a-Rolling" that used 220 performers and 800 costumes to trace the history of transportation on a 450-foot stage.

Walt decided he wanted a little company. He invited along animator Ward Kimball. Like Walt, Kimball was a kid at heart. He had a big enough collection of mechanical toys to fill a warehouse. A witty, imaginative man, he had come to work for Disney in April, 1934, and gone on to design a number of classic characters, including Jiminy Cricket.

"In the mornings we'd go down there and the locomotives would be worked on, getting greased and ready for the first performance," recalled Kimball. "They let us run them. We were like little kids, running famous locomotives like the Lafayette, the John Bull, and the Tom Thumb." Tooting train whistles made Walt happier than collecting an armful of Oscars.

Walt's curiosity was boundless—and not just about the trains. He scanned the flow of people from one exhibit to another, and wondered whether the paths could have been planned better. He closely watched the short-order chefs to see how they prepared hamburgers.

At night, Kimball wanted to go hear some of the famous jazz musicians who played in Chicago. But Walt had other ideas. He dragged Kimball along on lengthy excursions on the elevated trains to see places he'd visited as a teenager. "He'd be looking out the window and reliving his childhood," said Kimball.

After the fair, Walt bought model trains for his young nephews. He built towns and villages and even trees to go around the tracks. The boys absolutely loved their presents. But Walt couldn't spend all his spare time making models for kids. He was a grown man, after all.

*Walt delighted in sharing his interests—whether in miniatures or anything else—with his two daughters Sharon and Diane.*

© Walt Disney Enterprises

No, Walt wanted a train for himself.

When he and Lilly decided to buy a new house in 1949, Walt insisted that it have enough property for its own half-mile circle of one-eighth size train tracks. After a few discussions, Walt wrote up a legal-sounding contract which said, in part, "Whereas Walt and Lillian are husband and wife and Diane and Sharon are their children, in which family there presently exists an atmosphere of love . . . the aforesaid Lillian, Diane, and Sharon . . . assign and set over to Walt all their right, title, and interest in and to the right of way."

The tracks, which wound through the fruit trees on his property, included a tunnel that was 120 feet long, shaped like an S. Riders couldn't see the end when they started going through. When one of the construction workers told Walt that it would be cheaper to build the tunnel straight, Walt looked at him with amusement. "No," he said. "It's cheaper not to do it at all."

Walt's train, when completed, was a steam-driven beauty painted black with red-and-gold trim. On weekends, Walt invited visitors for a spin around the property with him as engineer. "It's my pride and joy, and I simply love it," Walt said.

The new house reflected Walt's personality in other ways. Not huge, it featured a playroom, a movie theater, and a soda fountain. Walt mixed the most hideous mile-high concoctions in the world, including champagne ice cream sodas, often decorated with tiny umbrellas sticking out of the cherry on top.

To anyone watching Walt in those days, it seemed he was pulling back—that he might even have retirement on his mind. For the first time in years, he had nonwork hobbies. Some of the enormous energy that was usually lavished on work went into his train, and a growing interest in miniatures. Sneaking away from his office, he would often drop by the machine shop at the studio and work side by side with his employees. With great care, he designed the decorative trimming for tiny tables and chairs, bringing new pieces to the dinner table at night to show off his work.

In the summer of 1949, he took his family to Europe, where *Treasure Island* was being filmed. They spent five weeks in England, a few days in Ireland, and three weeks in France and Switzerland. One afternoon, Walt came back to the family's hotel in Paris with boxes and boxes full of windup toys: monkeys that beat on drums and dogs that rolled over. He wound them all up, put them on the floor of the room and watched intently. "Isn't that amazing," he said to no one in particular. "Look at that movement, with just a simple mechanism. Look at that."

His children thought he was daft. They didn't realize that he was really studying these little mechanical toys, storing away what he learned for future use.

The trip was a happy one. Walt had a ball showing off the sights he had seen in the Red Cross. He was determined to use his limited French as much as possible; unfazed even when he accidentally ordered fried camel in a French restaurant.

In England, watching the movie being filmed, he was like a little boy with a new toy. He took great pleasure in the ease with which live-action films were made compared to the painstaking effort in cartoons. "These actors are great," he later teased his animators. "You give 'em the lines, they rehearse a couple of times and you've got it on film—it's finished. You guys take six months to draw a scene."

He enjoyed watching artists, like British-born Peter Ellenshaw, paint backgrounds. Called "mattes," these paintings made it possible to show a harbor,

Copyright © 1998 by Universal City Studios, Inc. Courtesy of Universal Studios Publishing Rights. All Rights Reserved

*W*alt Disney's first successful characters: Oswald the Rabbit, TOP, and Mickey Mouse. Though Walt would lose the rights to produce Oswald cartoons, Mickey would become the bedrock of the Disney empire. BELOW, Mickey stars in "The Band Concert," his first color cartoon.

© Walt Disney Enterprises

© Walt Disney Enterprises

© Walt Disney Enterprises

*A*lways an innovator, Walt was rewarded with two Academy Awards for his shorts "Flowers and Trees" (1932), a **Silly Symphony** (TOP), and "Three Little Pigs" (1933). Here the Pigs introduce their hit song "Who's Afraid of the Big Bad Wolf?"

© Walt Disney Enterprises

***S**now White and the Seven Dwarfs* *was another successful innovation. Originally dubbed "Disney's Folly," this first animated feature-length movie would prove a box-office hit.* TOP, *Snow White meets the Seven Dwarfs,* FROM LEFT: *Dopey, Sneezy, Happy, Grumpy, Doc, Bashful, and Sleepy.* BELOW, *the Evil Queen's appearance as the witch had audiences on the edge of their seats.*

© Walt Disney Enterprises

© Walt Disney Enterprises

*T*he evolution of Mickey Mouse, ABOVE. *Following Mickey's successful introduction, Walt added other stars to his roster,* RIGHT. CLOCKWISE FROM TOP: *Mickey's girlfriend, Minnie; Donald Duck; Goofy, originally called Dippy Dawg; and Pluto,* BELOW, *shown here in a still from "The Pointer."*

© Walt Disney Enterprises

© Walt Disney Enterprises

© Walt Disney Enterprises

© Walt Disney Enterprises

Walt Disney continued to push the boundaries of animation with **Pinocchio** (1940) and **Bambi** (1942). **Pinocchio** involved the most technically and artistically complex animation ever attempted. TOP, the famous results of Pinocchio's lie. BELOW, an animation cel of Honest John and Gideon.

© Walt Disney Enterprises

© Walt Disney Enterprises

***B**ambi* shifted animation's direction from fantasy to realism, while keeping the strong story and characterization that were Disney's hallmarks. LEFT, *Bambi's mother strips bark for food.* BELOW, *Bambi encounters Thumper—and ice.*

© Walt Disney Enterprises

© Walt Disney Enterprises

$M$*ickey stars in "The Sorcerer's Apprentice" segment of* **Fantasia** *(1940),* TOP. *One of Walt Disney's most ambitious works, this combination of classical music and animation originally did not win critical or audience approval.* BELOW, *a scene from* **Dumbo**. *Completed during the studio strike and released later that year, it exceeded all expectations by becoming an overnight hit.*

© Walt Disney Enterprises

a castle, or anything else in a scene without a cameraman venturing anywhere near that site. Many of the beautiful waterfronts in *Treasure Island* never existed anywhere but on canvas. "Don't forget, guys, we don't need to go on location," Walt said, only half-joking, "because Peter here, he can paint an island."

In the future, Walt's animators would have to work hard to get his attention. The excitement of being on a movie set had him hooked. (As one artist joked, "As soon as Walt rode on a camera crane, we knew we were going to lose him.")

But there were other plans forming in his mind as well. Walt's playing was about to lead him down an entirely new path.

# Walt's Dream Kingdom

*"I happen to be a kind of inquisitive guy and when I see things I don't like, I start thinking why do they have to be like this and how can I improve them."*
—WALT DISNEY

© Walt Disney Enterprises

The voyage that ended with the opening of Disneyland in 1955 really began when he was entertaining his little girls on Sundays in the early 1940s. As the children took their fifteenth ride around the merry-go-round, Walt would sit quietly on a wooden bench, wondering why no one had invented a clean safe place where parents and children could enjoy themselves at the same time. Typical 1940s amusement parks were dilapidated places with rusty Ferris wheels, creaky merry-go-rounds, and a smell of rancid food in the air.

Just before the Second World War, Walt considered building a little amusement park of his own across the street from the studio for guests and employees. It would have pony rides, a train, and statues of Snow White, Mickey, and Minnie. Walt walked around the site, pacing it off, as people do when they are decorating a new house.

The idea never got off the ground, but Walt never forgot about it.

In the early 1950s, Walt played with various ideas for nonfilm entertainment. In 1951, for instance, he helped studio artists and carpenters build a perfect miniature cabin complete with lamps, dishes, and a view of a vegetable garden with tiny carrots. He displayed the cabin at a home show in the Pan-Pacific

114

Auditorium. It was such a success that Walt developed plans for a whole series of similar nostalgic scenes for a travelling show that would tour around the United States. "He didn't want poor people to have to come clear across the country and stay at a hotel," said Harper Goff, a studio artist. "He wanted it to go to the people."

As Walt's ideas advanced, however, it became clear to him that a travelling show could never make any money. Its small size would prevent enough people from watching at one time.

He turned his attention to building a "family park," unlike any amusement park. There would be no Ferris wheel or roller coaster. Visitors wouldn't be afraid to eat the food. Admission would be charged—"If I don't, there can be drunks and people molesting people in the dark rides," he said.

Every place he went, he explored, questioned, and developed his plan. On a visit to Europe, Walt was terribly excited by the Tivoli Gardens in Copenhagen, Denmark. It was reasonably priced and guests were treated well. Most important, it was immaculate. He wanted to make his park sparkle like that.

© Walt Disney Enterprises

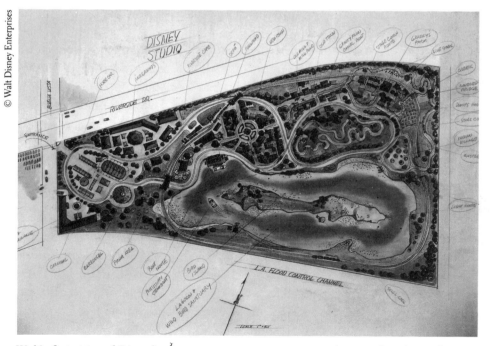

*Walt's first vision of Disneyland was an amusement area across the street from his studio.*

*Walt picked up Oscars for four individual productions in 1954:* The Living Desert; The Alaskan Eskimo; Toot, Whistle, Plunk and Boom; *and* Bear Country.

Academy Awards® Photograph Copyright of the Academy of Motion Picture Arts and Sciences.

"Women don't want to take their children into dirty rest rooms," he said.

From coast to coast, amusement-park owners told him that he was off his rocker.

"You can't charge admission," they claimed. "You have to have a Ferris wheel. . . . You've got to serve liquor. . . . It will cost you too much money to keep clean rest rooms. . . . You're going to lose your shirt."

Roy, too, was opposed. As far as he was concerned, Walt should stay in the studio where he was needed, not go gallivanting around playing at amusement parks. Roy felt a deep responsibility to his stockholders, even if that meant saying no to his brother. He told Walt that he wouldn't provide the cash for his latest whim. "We're in the motion-picture business," he said. "We're in the animated-film business. We don't know anything about this entertainment business. I don't look at that as a very good omen."

To be sure, there was plenty to keep Walt occupied back at the studio. *Cinderella*, which came out in 1950, was a big hit, but *Alice in Wonderland* took a "nose dive," in Walt's words, when it was released in 1951. "There was no heart to it," he explained to interviewer Pete Martin several years later. *Peter Pan*, which was released two years later, did better at the box office, but was no blockbuster.

Meanwhile, the True-Life Adventure films had been so successful that the

116

studio embarked on several feature-length documentaries. When RKO again balked, the Disneys set up their own distribution company, called Buena Vista. Another live-action film, *The Story of Robin Hood*, came out in 1952, followed by other semihistorical movies. The studio was also embarking on its most ambitious film project to date, *20,000 Leagues Under the Sea*, which was jammed with special effects and cost more than $4 million to make.

The directors and producers of all these projects were anxious to get Walt's attention—in hopes that he could lend a bit of his unique talent for making bold improvements. When he was dissatisfied with the squid attack scene in *20,000 Leagues Under the Sea*, for example, he had the sequence reshot. "Add a storm," he ordered. Those three words cost the studio $250,000, and left the soundstage soggy for years. But the picture was vastly improved.

Already, Walt slept only a few hours a night. But he was dead set on his park, and he wasn't going to let anything or anyone stop him. Even Roy.

If the company wasn't going to back him, he'd use his own money. He cleaned out his small savings accounts. He borrowed $100,000 against his life insurance. He sold his vacation home in Palm Springs. He persuaded dozens of employees to loan him money.

Lilly was not thrilled at seeing their life savings gambled. But there was no stopping Walt. "I couldn't ever see that there was any better place to put money than in the thing I was interested in," he said.

In December, 1952, he started Walt Disney, Incorporated, which later became WED Enterprises (for Walter Elias Disney). This firm would take charge of designing and building Disneyland. It would be a creative place staffed with "Imagineers"—designers, architects, engineers, writers, and artists, who would be given a free hand to develop new ideas and technological advances. Walt was the only stockholder.

WED would give Walt something he had desired for years—a small company that he could really control; where he could make decisions without the interference of accountants, bankers, and investors. Walt came to relish the hours he spent at WED—people who knew him from the studio detected that he was unusually relaxed when he was brainstorming with his imagineers. They called it Walt's "laughing place," a reference to the tune from *Song of the South*.

He hired the Stanford Research Institute to help him figure out where the park should be located. After an extensive study of Southern California, the researchers suggested Anaheim. The climate was good. It was close to the free-ways. Enough land was available.

Now Walt had a team of designers and a place to put the park. Only one thing was stopping him. This dream was going to cost millions of dollars and he had run out of money again.

Fortunately, he had an idea for raising all the money he needed.

# On the Air

© Walt Disney Enterprises

*"Instead of considering television a rival,
when I saw it, I said 'I can use that.'
Television is an open sesame to many
things. I don't have to worry about going
out and selling the theater man. . . . I go
directly to my public."*
—WALT DISNEY

Walt was intrigued with the possibilities of television long before most people had heard of it. From the late 1930s, he had been trying to get involved in this new small-screen entertainment; he even considered buying a television station at a time when Los Angeles had only one channel.

In the early 1950s, other film producers regarded the new medium, which they called "the monster," with suspicion, fearing that it would keep audiences out of the movie theaters. Walt disagreed. He recognized that television gave him the chance to come into his audience's homes and promote his work.

In 1950, Walt's face was first seen smiling from many of the 4.4 million TV screens in America. This show, "One Hour in Wonderland," sponsored by Coca-Cola, was the first time a major movie studio had produced a televison program. Set in a Christmas party at the studio, it mostly consisted of segments from Walt's *Alice in Wonderland*, which was to be released in a few months. The following year, he happily did another Christmas show, sponsored by Johnson & Johnson.

119

The need to raise money for Disneyland gave Walt the last shove he needed to go into television in a big way. In 1953, networks paid lots of money for big names like Bob Hope and Jack Benny. If someone wanted his name enough, Walt figured they might help finance his park. Moreover, a national show would give Disneyland free publicity.

For the first time since Walt had started talking about Disneyland, Roy thought his brother was making some sense. Finally, the younger brother was thinking about ways to raise money for his projects—not just coming up with new projects. Roy agreed to go to New York to negotiate with the networks. "What do we have for them to look at that will really grab their attention?" he asked Walt.

That was a problem. Walt and his designers were chock-full of terrific ideas for the park. But there was nothing dramatic on paper.

So, on a Saturday morning in September, 1953, Walt asked Herb Ryman, a former Disney artist and good friend of the family, to join him at the studio. Walt envied Ryman because the artist had recently spent months travelling with the Ringling Brothers Circus, painting their activities. An incredibly versatile painter and designer, Ryman was like Walt in his boundless curiosity. He was all ears when Walt told him the plans for Disneyland and explained that Roy was leaving for New York on Monday to raise money for the park.

"I sure hope he gets it," said Ryman. "But what did you want to see me about?"

"You know how these bankers are, Herbie. They can't visualize anything. They're just thinking about money. My brother's got to take drawings and plans to show what we're going to do."

"Well, naturally," said the unsuspecting Ryman. "I want to see them. Where are they?"

Walt pointed a long finger. "You're going to do them. This weekend."

"I'm not going to do anything in two days," he said. "You're crazy. . . . You've got a lot of nerve to call on me on Saturday, hoping I can come up with something. . . . Well, I can't. . . . Nobody in the world can do it . . . It will embarrass me and you. . . . I don't want anything to do with it. . . . We're still good friends, but that's impossible."

Two hours later, Ryman had started working. The two men stayed up all Saturday night. Walt talked as Ryman drew. By Sunday night, they had finished a full-color, heavily detailed drawing of the park.

The artwork showed Main Street leading up to a circular path (the hub). Streets coming out of the hub, like spokes on a wheel, led to Holidayland, Mickey Mouse Club, Frontier Country, Fantasyland, the World of Tomorrow, Recreationland, and other attractions. Obviously, many of these early ideas never actually made it into the park.

Roy took Ryman's work in hand and went to New York. CBS was totally uninterested. NBC was interested, but not willing to commit. Only ABC— by far the littlest of the three networks—was ready to sign on the dotted line. Leonard Goldenson, president of ABC, thought that Walt Disney's reputation could help put his network on the map. CBS had "I Love Lucy," Ed Sullivan, and Jackie Gleason. NBC had Sid Caesar and Bob Hope. Now, ABC could have Walt Disney.

A deal was struck. Walt would provide a one-hour weekly series to ABC. He would also give ABC one-third ownership in the park. In exchange, ABC would put up $500,000 in cash and guarantee $4.5 million in loans.

In early 1954, Roy decided to put the corporation's money into the park. He was persuaded that stockholders would be well rewarded for their involvement in Disneyland. With ABC's money, and an investment from the company that produced Disney comics and books, Walt had the cash he needed to get his dream off the drawing board.

As Walt concentrated on putting together ideas for his new show, Diane brought him the news that she wanted to get married. Her love was another student at the University of Southern California, where she went to college— a handsome football player named Ron Miller. Walt described him in a letter to his brother Herb as "a wonderful boy, a big athlete whom we all love."

Diane and Ron got married in a tiny church in Santa Barbara, California. At the reception, Walt stood on tiptoe when the photographers snapped photographs of him with his new son-in-law. Otherwise, Walt would have seemed like a pygmy alongside six-foot-five Ron.

On October 27, 1954, "Disneyland"—he had named the new show after the park—was on the air. Much of the program was filmed in color in spite of the fact that it would be broadcast in black-and-white. Once again, Walt showed startling foresight. "He looked into the future," said his son-in-law, Ron Miller. "He shot in color because he knew that the day was going to come, not too far in the future, when television would be color."

Walt discovered much of his film and cartoon work could be recycled for

121

use on television. The quality he had insisted on was paying off. The show was a mixture of fantasy, adventure, education, and drama. In addition, Walt made regular televised reports about the building of Disneyland, getting people excited about the park before it opened.

Walt was master of ceremonies. The little boy who had dreamed of becoming a famous star with his buddy Walt Pfeiffer finally saw that wish come true. "I was dying for somebody to suggest my doing that job," he said.

From the beginning, there were battles with advertisers who tried to tell Walt what to do. This was not unusual at the time. Sponsors had a great deal of power to control exactly what people saw on television. Cigarette companies made sure that only the good guys smoked on the programs they paid for. On one show, sponsored by Ford, the Chrysler building was actually painted out of the New York skyline.

Fortunately, Walt was powerful enough to do his show on his terms. "There is nobody, you see, that can tell me yes or no," he said. "If I make a stinky program, or it collapses, it's gonna be me."

The number of stinky programs was few. For three years, "Disneyland" was the only ABC show in the top fifteen rated programs. "Davy Crockett"—"king of the wild frontier"—was filmed in three one-hour segments and was an enormous hit the first season. "It was the first time television produced a miniseries," recalled Fess Parker, the actor who became an instant star portraying the frontiersman. By the time the television shows were combined into a feature film, nearly every seven-year-old in the country owned a coonskin cap and could recite the words of the show's theme song.

Over the next few years, "Davy Crockett" was followed by other highly successful programs including "Zorro," the story of a Spanish-Californian hero who slashed the letter Z onto the shirts of numerous bad guys with his sword.

The "Man in Space" episode, which aired in 1955, used information supplied by scientist Wernher Von Braun and others to give viewers a glimpse into the possibilities for spaceflight, including landing on the moon. Animation and live documentary footage were both used. Many of the ideas discussed on the show later became reality.

This was truly remarkable: The U.S. government didn't start its own space program until 1960.

# One Brick at a Time

*"It's kind of fun to do the impossible."*
—WALT DISNEY

Disneyland was the biggest project Walt had ever undertaken. He committed himself to building the park in just about two years. In that time he had to turn 180 acres of orange groves into a magic kingdom complete with a turn-of-the-century Main Street, a castle, a jungle, a riverboat, a railroad line, restaurants, walkways, ticket booths, and rest rooms.

Almost every day Walt was at the park, watching, correcting, arguing, and instructing. "Move this tree six feet to the left," he'd command.

Slowly, out of the mud, bits and pieces of the final product emerged. The layout was an inspired departure from traditional amusement parks that consisted of one long boulevard. Main Street led to the hub, where Sleeping Beauty Castle was located. The hub, in turn, led to Fantasyland, Adventureland, Frontierland, and Tomorrowland. When a guest reached the entrance to any land, he would immediately see an enticing attraction that would draw him forward like a hotdog at the end of a stick. Walt called these people-magnets "wienies."

Every day, attractions were added or cut or changed. Sketches were done, then models, so that Walt could properly visualize the concepts. Many of the designers had a background in film and used tricks they learned on movie sets to create illusions. One device was called "forced perspective." Because the upper floors of buildings on Main Street were in a smaller scale than the first, the eye was fooled into thinking the structures were taller than they really were.

"The first scheme you had, Walt would completely tear apart," said Marvin Davis, an original Disneyland designer who carefully mapped out 129 different plans for the entryway to the park. "Eventually, you would come up with something better. He wanted to see every idea that you could possibly have before he settled on something."

Many ideas never made it. Rock Candy Mountain was supposed to be a candy-studded walk-through attraction for small children. Unfortunately, it turned out that an entire mountain made of gooey sweet stuff was pretty sickening. "The model got more nauseating as we went," said Imagineer John Hench. "So we thought maybe the artificial candy was looking kind of dumb. We brought in a lot of real candy and chocolate and a whole bunch of gumdrops for trees. We didn't have air-conditioning and so the whole thing began to

*Main Street, U.S.A. in Disneyland, an idealized version of Marceline, Missouri, under construction.*

melt. Then birds flew in and pecked the gumdrops off." Finally, Walt gave in and killed the ride.

No attraction that made it into the park was more ambitious than the Jungle Cruise. A river had to be built in the middle of Anaheim and populated with animals and exotic vegetation. Landscaper Bill Evans was faced with the task of building the jungle; there wasn't the time to grow one. He drove around the area, searching for "character" trees that were particularly interesting. He even created whole new life forms, by turning trees upside down so that their roots were up in the air; then he'd grow vines on the roots.

Walt was talked out of getting live animals to populate his river. The monkeys and elephants would have to be fed, for one thing. They might run away or sleep during the heat of the day when guests were visiting. People would get different quality rides—one person might see dozens of animals, while another would see none. Mechanical beasts were the only solution.

As it turned out, they were sometimes just as fickle as the real ones. Crocodiles coated with mud ground to a stop. The giraffe, chewing on a leaf, kept getting his mouth stuck. The animals were powered with water pressure—Walt was afraid that some child might electrocute himself if electricity were used—and so they were irregular in their movements. If too many people in

© Walt Disney Enterprises

125

*The bronze plaque commemorating opening day still welcomes visitors to Disneyland. While the opening was a disaster, the park would grow to fulfill its promise.*

© Walt Disney Enterprises

Anaheim took a bath on Sunday night, the water pressure dropped, and the elephants looked like somebody had given them a sleeping pill. (The animals were later animated with electricity.)

Walt and his crew worked fifteen and eighteen hours a day. Opening day approached. Estimated costs for Disneyland had soared to $17 million and still it looked like the park wouldn't be ready. Nothing was working in Tomorrowland; Rocket to the Moon was still on the launchpad. Heavy rains had turned much of the park into muddy swamps. Labor unions were striking—in some cases even destroying work they had completed in order to intimidate their Disneyland employers.

On July 13th, with the opening just a few days away, Walt and Lilly celebrated their 35th anniversary at the park. After mint juleps on the *Mark Twain* sternwheeler, the guests went to the Golden Horseshoe for dinner. For a few hours Walt forgot the pressure and tension of the park and had a good time. A very good time. He had a drink in his hand from the moment the evening began.

Sitting with Sharon and Diane at their table, Lilly suddenly realized she didn't know where Walt had gone to. Then she found out. There he was, hanging over the balcony of the restaurant, shouting "bang-bang" at the stage.

The audience applauded him a bit, and he got downstairs and went onto the stage where he was joined by his family. Soon everybody was dancing. Walt loved every minute of it.

Diane decided that it would be best if she drove him home. Walt sat in the backseat of the car clutching a rolled-up map of Disneyland. Recalled Diane, "He was tooting through it like a little boy with a toy trumpet. And then he was singing a song. And before I knew it, there he was like a little boy, sound asleep, with his trumpet folded in his arms."

# Black Sunday

*"Daddy wanted his opening to be perfect."*
—SHARON DISNEY

© Walt Disney Enterprises

There was no moon the night of Saturday, July 16, 1955. With the opening just a few hours off, dozens of men and women sweated and swore in the dark, humid park as they feverishly labored to get ready.

Men waded through the Jungle Cruise river, hefting a 900-pound mechanical elephant into place. Plumbers welded pipes together to get rest rooms operating. Painters madly splashed colors where raw surface showed. Maintenance men spread banners and balloons all around Tomorrowland to hide the fact that nothing was operating there.

Walt, who had been up almost all night working, would have postponed the opening if he could. But a live television show had been scheduled for months. When the gates of the park opened, he watched from the window of his private apartment over the firehouse. Crowded around him were the Mouseketeers, two dozen talented teens and pre-teens, who were about to make their debut as Disney performers.

When the first children raced into the park, Mouseketeer Sharon Baird, age 12, looked at her new employer. "It must have been quite a feeling for him," she said. "I remember seeing the tears in his eyes."

128

Afterwards, Walt descended to read the dedication, which visitors to Disneyland can still find on a bronze plaque in the Town Square. *To all who come to this happy place, welcome. Disneyland is your land. Here age relives fond memories of the past and here youth may savor the challenge and promise of the future. Disneyland is dedicated to the ideals, the dreams and the hard facts that have created America—with the hope that it will be a joy and inspiration to all the world.*

In the parade that followed, a happy but nervous Walt rode in a car next to the governor of California, while the band played "Stars and Stripes Forever."

The rest of the day was chaos. Walt was a blur, racing from one attraction to another, checking in with employees, reading dedications for the different "lands" and doing interviews for the live 90-minute television broadcast "Dateline Disneyland." His involvement with the show—hosted by Art Linkletter, Bob Cummings, and future president (then actor) Ronald Reagan—temporarily shielded him from the knowledge that his opening was a disaster.

In fact, just about everything went wrong. The opening was supposed to have been "by invitation only." But thousands of fake invitations had been mysteriously distributed. On Sunday, the roads leading to Disneyland were jammed with beeping drivers impatient to get out of their hot cars. Once they all arrived, the park was overloaded. And unfinished.

Walt would later call the day "Black Sunday."

There were too few trash cans; the park was soon covered with garbage. The heat of the day melted the newly laid asphalt; dozens of startled women left their high heels behind in the sticky stuff. Rides broke down. Lines to the Jungle Cruise snaked out endlessly in the hot summer sun. So many passengers got on the *Mark Twain* at once that it sank low in the water, flooding its lower deck. There weren't enough water fountains.

"People said that we hadn't put in enough drinking fountains because we were trying to make money selling soft drinks," said Ron Dominguez, then a new Disney employee, later Executive Vice President of Disneyland. "That wasn't the reason. When they ran out of time, they had to choose between putting in rest rooms or water fountains. They chose the rest rooms."

Only there weren't enough working rest rooms, either.

The TV cameras fixed on things that looked good: the opening parade and convocation, rousing band music, Frank Sinatra, Sammy Davis, Jr., and other celebrities driving around in miniature cars, and generally having a high time. But even the telecast had problems. Microphones went dead and cameras caught Walt on the air when he wasn't expecting to be seen.

The next several days, he read newspaper accounts of the hideous opening. "It felt like a giant cash register," one critic said, "clicking and clanging as creatures of Disney magic came tumbling down from their lofty places in my daydreams to peddle and perish their charms with the aggressiveness of so many curbside barkers. . . ."

Walt's response to such criticism was predictable; he took it as a challenge to prove himself right. As for newspaper critics: "They're odd creatures . . . ," he said. "I say, to hell with them."

130

# Why? Because We Like You!

© Walt Disney Enterprises

*"We kids were told to address him as Uncle Walt—that's what he requested. But I couldn't do that. I had so much respect for him that it stayed Mr. Disney forever."*
—ANNETTE FUNICELLO
*Mouseketeer*

*The proposed Mickey Mouse Club Circus at Disneyland*

Viewers who tuned in to the opening day of Disneyland might not have understood what they were seeing when twenty-four young performers wearing cowboy hats were introduced as "The Mousketeers."

A few months later, everyone in America knew these children. On October 3, 1955, "The Mickey Mouse Club" premiered on ABC. Within weeks, pretty Annette, wide-grinned Bobby, and cute little Cubby were celebrities. The program's theme song—"M-I-C (see you real soon) K-E-Y (Why? because we like you!)"—became an anthem for a whole generation.

The idea had actually come from ABC. Happy with the success of Walt's first show, the network promised him another $1.5 million for the park if he would do a kid's program to compete with "Howdy Doody."

Bill Walsh, a gifted writer and producer, was put in charge. Though a daily program was terribly demanding for everyone, the Disney animation libraries helped him fill the hour. By 1955, the studio was producing only a handful of cartoons, but more children would see the old Mickey Mouse and Donald Duck shorts on television than had ever seen them in movie theaters.

131

THE MAN BEHIND THE MAGIC

In March, Walt decided to call the stars of the show Mouseketeers. He and Walsh hired Jimmie Dodd, a cheerful 45-year-old, and Roy Williams, a heavyset animator and writer, to be their leaders. It was Williams who came up with the very first Mickey Mouse hats.

The search for the Mouseketeers themselves took several months. Hundreds of children from around the country were interviewed. Walt knew exactly what he wanted—not practiced Hollywood professionals, but ordinary kids. He sat in on many of the auditions. Annette Funicello, then 12, was the last of the original 24 children chosen. She had never sung in public before and remembered shaking like a leaf when Walt asked her to sing him a song. "I was very comfortable with the dancing, but not the singing," she said. "He made light of it, and was so kind. I felt such warmth from him."

Meanwhile, work began on several running serials—like "Spin and Marty," the story of two boys at a dude ranch—which would be shown as part of the hour show. Tim Considine, who played the likeable and very cool Spin, had absolutely no idea of Walt's plan to combine his series into the larger Mouse Club format. One day when he was hanging around the studio, the 14-year-old saw the "mice," as he always called them, for the first time.

"I remember seeing these strange little creatures with these ears and their names written across their front," Considine recalled. "I followed them to a little stage where they were rehearsing. That was the first time I ever saw the Mouseketeers. I remember being horrified because they were so talented and I didn't know how to do any of that."

By the time the show hit the air, a format had been established. Each day would have a different theme: Monday was Fun with Music Day, Tuesday was Guest Star Day, and so on. There was educational material, drawing lessons, travelogues, and cartoons, in addition to the regular serials.

"It was like a Chinese fire drill . . . ," Bill Walsh said in the *Mickey Mouse Club Scrapbook*. "We'd have meetings in the mornings with the kids, then we'd meet with the writers, then with the guy who did the sets and the costumes. After lunch, everyone would meet again. By that time, we all would contribute ideas about props, sets, wardrobe, music, and about three o'clock that afternoon we'd shoot it."

From the beginning, the show was immensely successful. At 5 P.M., Monday through Friday, three out of every four television sets in use in the United States were tuned to "The Mickey Mouse Club." Fan mail rolled in. Annette—

the attractive idol of millions of young boys—got two hundred letters a day!

Walt stayed in the background, and the Mouseketeers looked upon him with a mixture of awe and fascination. When he was on the set, he seemed almost shy. "He used to wear khakis—work clothes—and he was very quiet," said Mouseketeer Sharon Baird. "I remember he used to go next door to help mix paints. He'd come from the paint department with paint on him."

Behind the scenes, Walt made sure there was little swearing on the set— in sharp contrast to other studios where children worked. "I had been on other sets, and Disney was different," said Tommy Cole, who was 13. "It was like a home. It was like a family. You didn't find a lot of rowdy people."

There was pressure. All were pushed to do their best—and that sometimes resulted in tears. A number of Mouseketeers were dropped along the way, including Cole, who was released from his contract after the first season because of problems with his dancing, then picked up again before the second season when he practiced and improved. The Mouseketeers worked longer, harder schedules than most adults—including summers when they put in a full eight-hour day performing in a circus at the park. But there were many benefits. "We loved working out at Disneyland," said Sharon Baird. "We used to get to warm up the rides before the gate was opened."

"Walt made sure everything was always first-class," said Bobby Burgess, who was 13 when the program began. "He made sure we had our own sleeping car and dining car when we travelled places on the train. We had a ball."

Why the Mickey Mouse show went off the air at the end of four seasons remains something of a mystery. ABC claimed it was having difficulties getting enough sponsors for the program. Walt thought that it was losing popularity because it had too many commercials already.

Walt still had two shows on the network: "Disneyland" and "Zorro." But the conclusion of "The Mickey Mouse Club's" run in 1959 was the beginning of the end of Walt's long-standing relationship with ABC.

The "Disneyland" show had been beaten in the ratings by NBC's new western, "Wagon Train." ABC's response: Walt should make westerns. The tension between him and ABC grew.

Then, when "Zorro" was about to go into its third year on ABC, executives decided that they wanted to own a piece of the show themselves; they could make much more out of programs they owned than those produced by independents.

As Walt's nephew, Roy, remembered the story, ABC threatened to put the show on at two o'clock in the morning if the Disneys didn't cave in. "That made my father angry," said Roy, "and for the next year he prepared for a lawsuit. Then, before the case actually came to court, the president of ABC saw the light, and in his settlement he sold back the one-third of Disneyland that ABC owned."

It all turned out for the best. The Disneys had already bought out all the other investors in Disneyland, so now total control of the park was in their hands. What's more, they could now move to NBC—a network interested in using color on Walt's show. The investment Walt had made in shooting the program in color all along would pay off.

Meanwhile, Walt had retained at least part of "The Mickey Mouse Club." When the series ended, he signed a new contract with Annette Funicello, always the most popular Mouseketeer. Walt launched her on a movie and recording career.

"Remember, I can't sing," she said.

"We'll make you sound good. Don't worry about it," he responded.

Several years later, when she was graduating from high school, he wanted her to appear at Radio City Music Hall. At first she refused, wanting to stay home, but when Walt made a personal request, she consented. To make up for the fact that she missed her graduation, he arranged for the Superintendent of Schools of New York to present her with her diploma on the stage of Radio City, while the Rockettes were doing their high kicks.

"Isn't that the nicest graduation present anyone could ever have?" Annette said. "Who cares about a prom?"

# The Next Generation

© Walt Disney Enterprises

*"Instead of saying 'Dead End,' grandchildren say 'Through road.' "*
—ROY DISNEY

*Walt and his grandson, Christopher*

Some men fear that becoming a grandfather will make them old. Not Walt. Even though he was beginning to feel his age—an old polo injury had caused a painful form of arthritis in his neck—he was thrilled to be a grandfather.

His first grandson, Christopher, had come at the end of 1954. Walt stood in front of the crib, camera in hand, clicking pictures of every giggle and gurgle. "I can't tell you how much fun he is," the doting grandpa wrote Ruth. "We're all crazy about him."

Walt's only disappointment was that the child hadn't been named for him. "We were going to call the baby Walter," explained Diane, "and then I started thinking that I had to give him a new name. He was a new person. Afterward, I felt that we had made a mistake."

About seven months after Christopher was born, Diane was pregnant again. Walt set about personally designing a new house for Diane and her family. Evenings, while Lilly slept, he made sketches for the architects. He even considered setting up their kitchen as a sort of scientific laboratory, to test new work-saving devices.

When the news came in the middle of the night that Diane's second baby,

*As much as Walt was preoccupied with work, he loved to be surrounded by his family. From left to right are Ron, Sharon, Diane and Joanna, Lillian, and Christopher.*

© Walt Disney Enterprises

Joanna, had been born, Walt was thrilled. "Oh, a little girl," he groggily said to Lilly, "how wonderful for Ron. He'll love it. He'll love having a daughter." Then Walt lit a cigarette, pulled out the house plans, and said, "Now, let's get separate bathrooms for the children."

Another girl, Tamara, was born in 1957, and Walt, who was in Chicago at the time, sent a congratulatory telegram to "Tamara Walter Elias Disney Miller."

That year, Roy began catching up in the grandchild department. Roy Edward and his wife of two years, Patty, named their first son Roy Patrick, so there were now three Roys in the family. Two girls and another boy followed. The eldest Roy was a down-on-the-floor grandfather. Once Patty came home to find a big gash on her father-in-law's knee, a scrape on his head, and an ice pack on his elbow. He'd been playing kickball with the children.

Meanwhile, the second generation of Disneys was becoming a presence at the studio. Roy Edward Disney had begun working there in 1952. He resisted any idea that he might follow in his father's footsteps and become a businessman. He felt that he was cut out for the artistic side of things and worked on Walt's television show. He also wrote a number of nature films and was a photographer on *Perri*, a fanciful 1957 movie about a squirrel.

Uncle Walt made Roy work just as hard as any other up-and-coming young employee, if not harder. "He wasn't unfair to me," said Walt's nephew, "but on the other hand he expected one heck of a lot."

136

Ron Miller also had worked briefly for Walt before joining the army. Afterwards, he played football for the Los Angeles Rams for a season. Both times Walt went to see Ron play, Ron got injured. Once he was knocked cold. After the season Walt said to Ron, "You know, I've got three grandchildren by you. And if you keep playing football, you're going to die, and I'm going to have to raise those little guys."

So, Ron began working for his father-in-law again. He worked on films like *Old Yeller* (1957) and *Third Man on the Mountain* (1959). In time, he became an associate producer. "Walt thought of Ron as being his son," said family-friend Herb Ryman. "He would stand outside the studio, watching the cars come in and he'd explain to Ron who the various people were so that Ron would know how the business worked."

"I have great ambition for him," Walt said. "He will run the studio one day."

In March, 1959, out of the blue, Walt found himself doubled over with numbing pain deep in his lower back. The doctor made him check into the hospital immediately. His trouble was a kidney stone; one of the most excruciating conditions a man can suffer.

While he was still recovering in his hospital room, Sharon came by with Bob Brown, a bright young architect from Kansas City whom she had been seeing for a year and a half. They told Walt they wanted to get married. "Well, she's your problem now," Walt teased his son-in-law to-be.

Almost as soon as the two were wed, in May, Walt was urging them to provide him with more grandchildren. "We keep asking," Walt wrote to Ruth, only seven months after the wedding. "Maybe one of these days she'll surprise us."

# King of Disneyland

*"It has that thing—the imagination and the feeling of happy excitement—I knew when I was a kid."*

—WALT DISNEY

© Walt Disney Enterprises

The Disneys spent many nights in the park after it opened. Their apartment was over the fire station on Main Street, decorated by Lilly in typical Victorian style with ornate flower-patterned furniture, and rose-colored carpeting and drapes. Toys were kept handy in case a grandchild came to call. At night, the roar of wild animals from the nearby Jungle Cruise ride lulled them to sleep.

Walt had breakfast at Aunt Jemima's Pancake House and dinner at the Disneyland Hotel. "He practically lived there," said Lilly.

Television had made him easily recognized and he was mobbed for autographs whenever he was in the park. He loved the attention and the contact but soon realized that he wasn't getting anything done. So, he donned sunglasses and a floppy-brimmed hat as a disguise. When a child recognized him, and asked for an autograph, he put a finger to his lips to convey that this should be their secret. Then he reached into his pocket and pulled out a scrap of paper on which he had written his name in advance.

Though the park was an extraordinary success within months of opening, Walt decided that the key to keeping it up was constant improvement and change. "Disneyland will never be completed," he said.

Walt called his constant fiddling and fixing "plussing" and he loved it. "A live picture, once you wrap it up and turn it over to Technicolor . . . it's gone," he said. "I can't touch it. There are things in it I don't like, but I can't do anything about them." Not so the park. "Not only can I add things, but even the trees will keep growing. The thing will get more beautiful each year. And as I find out what the public likes, I can change it."

Walt got rid of the companies he had originally hired to provide food for his guests. People were complaining. "They don't expect to be in business here five and ten years from now and I do," he said of the restaurateurs. "They're trying to make a buck now."

When Walt first took over the food operation, he gave his money men a scare. "We have to feed people that come here," he told them. "But I don't want to make any money on food." Seeing their astonished expressions, he backed up. "Well, I don't mind breaking even. But one thing I want to tell you. Coffee is only worth a dime. As long as I run this park it's only a dime."

Walt realized the only way to keep quality high was to train his employees carefully. He called them cast members—as far as he was concerned he was putting on a giant show.

When Walt saw one of the conductors on the railroad line handle some guests rudely, he went to the man's boss. "See if you can't give that fellow a better understanding of the kind of business we're in," he told him. "See if you can't cheer him up. If he feels sour, he shouldn't work here. We are selling happiness."

Cleanliness was Walt's preoccupation. He rarely passed by a men's room without sticking his head in to make sure it was immaculate. "If we keep the place clean, the guests will respect it," he said.

No flaw escaped Walt's eagle eyes. Dick Nunis, who later became president of Disney's entire park operation, was running Adventureland in the park's early days. He recalled Walt finishing a trip on the Jungle Cruise and emerging in a black fury. The trip had taken four-and-a-half minutes. It was supposed to take seven minutes. "I couldn't tell if they were hippos or rhinos," Walt raged. "How would you feel if you paid to go to the movies and they cut the center reel out of the picture?"

After a few weeks—during which time Dick Nunis spent more time on the Jungle Cruise than he did on dry land—the attraction was operating to perfection.

*Walt had originally resolved there would be no roller coasters in his park, but the Matterhorn (under construction here) was far removed from traditional thrill rides. Walt loved riding with visitors, watching them get splashed at the end.* © Walt Disney Enterprises

*The expansion of Disneyland continued with "Pirates of the Caribbean," a boat ride through a pirate kingdom.*

Charts were kept on the attractions. The more popular rides would stay; ones with declining ridership would be improved; those that were neglected would be cut.

The Phantom Boats in Tomorrowland started service shortly after opening day. About half the time they conked out after leaving the dock and soon enough they were just memories. The Disneyland Stagecoach suffered a similar fate as did a brief effort at a Disneyland circus.

Other attractions were added. Dumbo Flying Elephants, 20,000 Leagues Under the Sea, and the Mike Fink Keel Boats were all in operation before the end of 1955. The next year, Storybook Land and Tom Sawyer Island were added.

Walt oversaw construction on the Island personally. After it opened, Tom Nabbe, a red-headed boy with freckles who sold the *Disneyland News* on Main Street, approached Walt. "I think I should be Tom Sawyer on the island," he said.

"I'll think about it," Walt answered.

For weeks, Tom approached Walt repeatedly. Walt debated whether a live boy would be better than a dummy who wouldn't ever leave the island for a hotdog. Finally, Walt agreed and Tom played Tom Sawyer for four years. He outgrew the role, but was still working for the company thirty years later.

In 1959, the park underwent its first big expansion since opening. Over $7 million was spent on the Submarine Voyage, Disneyland Monorail, and the biggest of them all, the 14-story Matterhorn Mountain bobsled ride. Walt had gotten the idea while making *Third Man on the Mountain*, the feature film about conquering the Matterhorn in 1865. Though he had maintained that there would be no roller coasters in his park, the Matterhorn would be to roller coasters as Snow White was to Oswald the Lucky Rabbit. Walt himself adored taking guests like Bob Hope, King Hussein of Jordan, and former-President Harry Truman in the four-person bobsleds and watching them get splashed when the ride came to an end.

Once Herb Ryman's mother was serving Walt a piece of pumpkin pie in her home. "Why don't you run for president?" she asked him. "You'd make a good president. And people love you. You could be elected."

"Why should I be president," Walt asked, "when I'm already King? I'm King of Disneyland."

# On Location

© Walt Disney Enterprises

*"All right. I'm corny. But I think there's just about a-hundred-and-forty-million people in this country that are just as corny as I am."*
—WALT DISNEY

*Walt on the set of* 20,000 Leagues Under the Sea

Walt and Roy often felt that the movie critics were gunning for them. Their dramas were attacked for being cloying and overly sentimental; comedies came under fire for their broad, sometimes silly situations. Even some of the kinder reviewers assumed that Disney movies were just kiddie shows. "These sophisticates turn their nose up at anything," Walt complained to Pete Martin. "They say it's childish. Well, what the hell is wrong with something being childish?"

Critics aside, Walt had an amazing track record at the box office. Basically, he just made movies he wanted to see himself. His fondness for history and nostalgia guided him to pioneering-family sagas and good adventure yarns with a historical backdrop. During the mid-to-late fifties, the studio came out with movies like *The Great Locomotive Chase* (1956), *Westward Ho, the Wagons!* (1956), and *Johnny Tremain* (1957). "Daddy thinks there's nothing more exciting than American history," Diane said at the time.

Likewise, his love for simple broad humor guided the studio to gag-oriented situational comedies like *The Shaggy Dog*, a 1959 tale of a teenager who turns into a pooch, and *The Absentminded Professor*, a 1961 Fred MacMurray picture

143

about an addled scientist who discovers a substance called flubber that makes cars fly. Walt admitted that he adapted cartoon gags and style. "I'm doing gags in there I've done in my cartoons. It's an offshoot of years of gagging."

Above all, Walt resolutely believed in the importance of a good story. He had a special ability to structure plots that would hold the attention of both young people and their parents. He tried to avoid ever talking down to children in his movies. As Walt told the *Kansas City Times* in 1956, "I remember when I was a kid and some adult would pat me on the head and say, 'Well, little man, how are you?' I always felt like I wanted to kick him right in the teeth. When we put on a show, we try to put the children right in the middle of it. We never discount their intelligence. We don't try to be frenetic and jump all around and say, 'Isn't that funny?' "

To the dismay of critics and writers, Walt thought nothing of adding his own personal touches to someone else's work. Even with an old classic like *Swiss Family Robinson*, which came out in 1960, he couldn't resist a cartoonlike approach. His sense of the audience told him that, played straight, *Swiss Family Robinson* might be stiff and moralistic. He altered the personality of the father, built up the love interest, and threw in enough gadgets and gags to fill several movies.

"I said let's do it the way we do it with Donald Duck," Walt explained, referring to the fight scene in which a family of six defeats hundreds of dopey pirates using coconut bombs, rolling logs, and a tiger trap. The rollicking adventure that featured tigers, elephants, monkeys, and snakes, delighted young viewers so much that Walt decided to make an attraction in Disneyland out of the film family's tree house.

Walt was always searching for new properties, and he often bought the rights to literary works long before anything was filmed. His conversations with writer P. L. Travers about *Mary Poppins*, which came out in 1964, began in the early 1940s. Other Disney films—like *Lady and the Tramp* (1955), *Darby O'Gill and the Little People* (1959), and *The Sword in the Stone* (1963)—also grew from stories, books, or promising characters that had caught Walt's eye as much as fifteen or twenty years before.

Like animated features, live-action films were mapped out on storyboards. Every detail was prepared in advance—before an actor ever put a foot on the set. As in the past, Walt had an impressive ability to take in the scenes of a movie and see what was wrong.

Major casting decisions always needed his stamp of approval. For the most important roles, he interviewed the actors or actresses himself—though the meetings were often startlingly informal. When Hayley Mills was suggested for the title role in *Pollyanna*, he flew to London. "We met him at the Dorchester Hotel," the actress remembered. "I had with me this miniature Pekingese and he was very attracted to this little white dog. He spent some time on the floor playing with it. He was very much operating on my level."

When the 12-year-old girl came to America with her parents to start filming *Pollyanna*, the first of six movies she would make for the studio during Walt's lifetime, she discovered she had joined a family "of extremely nice and hospitable people."

Staying at the Beverly Hills Hotel, Mills discovered that Walt had ordered her room stuffed with flowers, fruits, and sweets. He took her and her family on a complete personal tour of Disneyland, riding on all the rides with them. "The best part of it all was that he was so much a part of our own personal life," she said. "He was a very calm and gentle person and he became a friend."

*Hayley Mills made six movies for Walt during his lifetime, starting when she was twelve. He enjoyed her performances so much that he rushed each day to see the results of the previous day's filming.*

145

By the time a movie began shooting, Walt was a quiet force on the set. If filming was at the studio, he would drop by almost daily to watch. If the movie was shot at some other exotic spot (on location), he and Lilly often grabbed the chance for a little work-vacation. When a film was shot away from the studio, and Walt was unable to be there, he was never out of mind. "When I did films on location, like *In Search of the Castaways* or *The Moon-Spinners*, they had to stop shooting and call him personally if they wanted to make changes in how a scene was going to be shot," said Hayley Mills. "They had to verify that it was acceptable to him."

Unfortunately, as time went on Walt was chained to a too-fast production schedule that limited his involvement in a number of films. For each masterpiece there was a disasterpiece. *Ten Who Dared* (1960), *Kidnapped* (1960), *Babes in Toyland* (1961), and *In Search of the Castaways* (1962) were all disappointments.

When Walt simply didn't have the hours to devote to a film, his insistence on control became a curse, not a blessing. He couldn't bring his magic to the screen in every film—and he didn't allow the directors to substitute their own instincts for his own. "The films were very definitely Walt Disney productions," said Hayley Mills, "but that was a double-edged sword. It hampered directors to check that everything they did would be acceptable."

Ron Miller explained, "He was in a trap. He had built up a staff and distribution company and then he had to make enough product for that distribution company. In that situation, you have to make some pictures you don't believe one hundred percent in. You just hope something accidental might happen to make them come out a little better than they went in."

*Sleeping Beauty*, the most expensive animated cartoon to date, lost money when it was released in 1959. The animation was intricate, detailed, and elaborate. But the plot and characters were far weaker than those in *Snow White* and *Cinderella*. Walt hadn't paid his usual attention to the story line, and hadn't checked in regularly with his artists. "You had to invite him in maybe a couple of times before he'd come," said Ollie Johnston, one of the "nine old men" and co-author with fellow "old man" Frank Thomas of several authoritative and entertaining books about animation. (The next animated feature, *One Hundred and One Dalmatians*, released in 1961, was charming and far more successful. Walt attributed the strength of the picture to the well-written book on which it was based.)

By the 1960s, Walt was "really beginning to get tired of films," said Diane. The outpouring of movies, both good and bad, had erased the company's debt. But success had locked Walt into a jail with golden bars. More and more Disney movies became rehashes of successful former efforts. He had long sworn that he would never make sequels, but *Son of Flubber,* released in 1963, was just that—a weak sister to *The Absentminded Professor.* After the tremendous success of *Old Yeller,* the heartbreaking story of a boy and his dog, in 1957, the studio churned out animal stories.

The man who had become famous by breaking all the rules was now imitating himself on the screen much of the time. To a great extent, the fault belonged to an audience that demanded predictable "Disney" fun from his features. A Disney movie had to be wholesome. It had to have clear-cut good guys and bad guys. The humor had to be easygoing and unsophisticated.

Break any of those rules, and the Disney audience screamed. When a man and woman drank martinis in the 1961 film *The Parent Trap,* the studio received hundreds of letters condemning the scandalous act. *Bon Voyage,* in 1962, featured a scene with a prostitute that drew even more angry letters.

"He was very frustrated," said Ron Miller. "Walt had created this image and he got locked in." In 1962, when he saw the movie, *To Kill a Mockingbird,* which dealt with prejudice in a small Southern town, he said, "Gee, I'd sure like to make a picture like that." But he was sure that the moviegoers of America would never stand for it.

# Walt and Roy

Photo credit: Rush Johnson

"If they hadn't been brothers, this thing would have fallen apart in the first ten minutes."
—ROY EDWARD DISNEY

*Walt and Roy visit Marceline*

The more things changed, the more they stayed the same.

After nearly forty years as a team, Walt and Roy were out of debt. They were both wealthy men. Yet the two were still squabbling the way they had when they were kids in Kansas City. Walt was tired of being treated like the foolish fifteen-year-old who had misplaced his soda bottles when he was working on the train. Roy was long weary of Walt's disregard for financial matters. Walt didn't go to stockholders' meetings. He wasn't on the board of directors. He had dropped all his official titles at the company.

"Titles or not," he said, "I'm still running this company." His formal relationship consisted of the stock he owned and a contract that provided for him to be paid for his services.

As always, the brothers' arguments were about money. When Walt decided that he wanted the studio to buy him a small airplane in 1963, for instance, Roy refused. What would the stockholders think about such a frivolous purchase?

Like a little boy with his heart set on a new bike, Walt insisted. "I need to travel places in a hurry," he said. "I can't always be making reservations.

148

Sometimes they don't even fly where I want to go. If the studio doesn't want to buy a plane for me, I'll buy it for myself!"

The studio bought Walt his plane.

One of the bigger blowups came when Roy decided that the studio should own WED. Not only was WED the creative arm of Walt's empire, it owned property, some rides at Disneyland, even the rights to profit from Walt's name. Roy was concerned that shareholders might think Walt was cheating them by favoring his personal company over the interests of Walt Disney Productions.

Walt didn't want to sell; WED was the one place where he didn't have to be accountable for the money he spent. Losing that freedom would be painful. "You know what they want now?" Walt fumed. "They want me to sell everything. They even want to buy my name from me. They think I should sell off my name!"

In the negotiations over WED, studio attorneys put a great deal of pressure on Walt—even threatening him with legal actions. That was too much for Roy. He heard that a meeting was going on in the conference rooms and stalked in.

"Look," he said, his eyes blazing. "You know we are all here right now because of Walt. My God, all of this is because of Walt. So, don't treat him as if he's some outsider we don't need around here. . . ."

Ultimately, Walt gave in, selling WED to the studio, though he did hang on to legal rights to the monorail and the steam train at Disneyland as well as profits that would come from the use of his name. There was another major compromise: By contract, WED had to be provided a large research budget to keep its creativity level high.

One of the battles between the two brothers dragged on for a while. Walt and Roy were negotiating over several important points in Walt's contract with the company. Walt was earning much less than other men in similar positions made. Out of the blue, Walt's lawyer confronted Roy with an astonishing statement. "Well, Roy," he said, "I guess I'm going to have to take my client and get a Hollywood agent to represent him!"

Roy turned beet red. He couldn't believe such a threat had been made. Of course, Walt would never have hired an outside agent—that was just a lawyer's trick. But it had the effect of turning a bad situation worse. Unkind words were said and before long the two brothers weren't talking with one another. This wasn't only hard on the two men. It hurt Lilly and Edna to see "the boys" arguing like this. For months, they communicated only through other people like Bill Cottrell, an intensely loyal, fair-minded man whose prime goal was to dampen the flames of battle between the two brothers.

The anger died down when Walt sent Roy a toy peace pipe for his birthday with the following note:

"It is wonderful to smoke the pipe of peace with you again. The clouds that rise are very beautiful. I think between us over the years we have accomplished something. . . . in all sincerity, happy birthday and many more—and—I love you."

# Mary Poppins

© Walt Disney Enterprises

*"I always wished that some of Walt's
magic would rub off on me."*
—DICK VAN DYKE

Every year, just before Christmas, Walt wrote a letter to his sister, Ruth, who
had remained in Portland. He'd fill her in on important events, and ask what
her son, Ted, might like for the holiday. On December 5, 1963, he wrote:
"We spent most of the summer here at the studio making *Mary Poppins* with
Julie Andrews, Dick Van Dyke, Ed Wynn, Glynis Johns, and two lovely little
English children, Karen Dotrice and Matthew Garber. We plan to release it
next Christmas, '64, and have high hopes for it. I think it's going to be one
of our best."

Walt was not disappointed.

His interest in P. L. Travers' book began in 1944, when he read eleven-
year-old Diane's copy. He and Roy sought out the author, but the relationship
was rocky from the start. Travers felt like Mary Poppins was a close personal
friend; Walt's desire to change the character and the story for a movie offended
her. For years, she resisted him. In 1960, she finally agreed—but only if she
were allowed to participate. Rancorous debates over changes in the story continued until the film was finished.

Walt himself was involved in every detail of this production. "It was his pet

151

*Walt kept "plussing" Mary Poppins with animation and elaborate visual effects. Karen Dotrice and Matthew Garber hang from invisible wires before a "blue screen." These scenes would later be combined with animated sequences.*

© Walt Disney Enterprises

project," Dick Van Dyke said. Enchanted by the tale of an English nanny who can talk to dogs, fly, jump through chalk drawings, and walk up smoke staircases, Walt's fatigue with films was completely absent on this particular set.

Julie Andrews, whom Walt had seen in the Broadway production of *Camelot*, was his pick for the star—though Travers worried that she was too pretty. Dick Van Dyke, one of the biggest television stars of the time, was selected to play the chimney sweep, Bert. Walt handpicked a staff for the movie: Bill Walsh was co-producer. The Sherman brothers, Richard and Robert, wrote the music. Robert Stevenson, who had directed *Old Yeller* and *The Absentminded Professor*, directed. Don DaGradi, one of Walt's best story men, handled the script.

Shortly after work started on the film, Walt asked Ron Miller to get a copy of *Song of the South*. A screening, with all the senior staff present, was arranged for that afternoon at two o'clock.

After they watched the live actors and cartoon characters on the screen, Walt said, "I just wanted to see something," got up and left.

Someone said, "Oh, my God. I hope he doesn't want animation in this picture." Nobody wanted *Mary Poppins* hoked up with cartoons. That would turn it into a kiddie movie, they thought.

The next day Walt called and asked to see the film again.

Tension choked the room after the clip was shown, until Walt spoke. "You know," he said, "I think this picture could use a little animation."

The assembled group took in this piece of information in shocked silence, except that "you could hear the Sherman brothers drop over dead," said Ron Miller.

The animated segments of *Mary Poppins* turned out to be some of the most enchanting in the picture.

Walt had no training in music—he couldn't even carry a tune—but he had an instinctive understanding of what he wanted in the movie's songs. He shook his head when the Sherman brothers first played "Supercalifragilistic-expialidocious" (people working on the film called it "Supercal"). "Something is wrong there," he said thoughtfully. "Why don't you try speeding it up a little bit?" It worked.

Walt's personal favorite was "Feed the Birds," a gentle song Mary Poppins sings about a kindly old woman in front of St. Paul's Cathedral. Evenings, after filming was done, Walt would relax in his office, trying to ignore the racking pain that now often assailed his back and neck. Often, he'd call the Sherman brothers in. "Play the song for me," he asked, and they knew, without asking, which one he wanted.

Throughout the filming, Walt kept "plussing" the picture. The nannies don't simply walk away from the Banks's home at the beginning of the movie; they are whisked away by the wind. The chimney sweeps' dance on the rooftops of London doesn't just end with a bow. Walt added fireworks to the finish.

As long as he could visualize a special effect—like a smoke staircase—he had absolute confidence that his team of wizards could make it appear on the screen. And woe to he who showed doubt or hesitation. "Walt did not like negative thoughts," said Peter Ellenshaw, the artist who painted many of the mattes which created the illusion of London in 1910. On one occasion Ellenshaw admitted to problems with a complicated rooftop dance sequence. He was met with a scowl that could melt iron. As Ellenshaw later realized, "I should have said 'There are problems, but golly we're going to have a lot of fun solving them!' "

By and large, the creation of the movie was amazingly smooth. Walt once remarked that he rarely saw a sad face around the studio during production. "This made me nervous," he joked. "I knew the picture would have to gross

A *still from the movie shows the finished effect*.

© Walt Disney Enterprises

ten million dollars for us to break even. But still there was no negative head-shaking. No prophets of doom. Even Roy was happy."

On August 27, 1964, *Mary Poppins* premiered in Hollywood. It received thirteen Academy Award nominations. Julie Andrews won as best actress. The film brought in some $44 million in its first release.

P. L. Travers was lukewarm. As Bob Thomas tells the story in *Walt Disney, an American Original*, she approached Walt at a joyous party after the premiere.

"Miss Andrews is satisfactory as Mary Poppins," she allowed. "But Mr. Van Dyke is all wrong, and I don't really like mixing the little cartoon figures with the live actors. When do we start cutting it?"

# A City of Tomorrow

© Walt Disney Enterprises

*"We keep moving forward, opening up new doors, and doing new things, because we're curious . . . and curiosity keeps leading us down new paths."*
—WALT DISNEY

*An early concept of EPCOT*

A shortage of money had stopped Walt from buying more land for Disneyland in the 1950s. Within a few years of opening, all manner of garish, un-Disneyland-like places surrounded it. Walt gritted his teeth and muttered when he drove down Harbor Boulevard to the park, past unsavory restaurants, cheap motels, and neon-lit tourist traps.

It was too late to do anything about the space crunch at Disneyland. So, beginning in the late 1950s, Walt's staff began looking for a possible location for a second park on the East Coast. Florida seemed likely. Land was cheap and it was warm all year. The coastline was out, though. Walt didn't want to risk hurricanes or people with wet bathing suits visiting his park.

As Walt's thoughts developed, the amusement-park aspect of his Florida Project, as it was called, receded in importance. A second Disneyland might be necessary to bring in visitors and money. But his true dream was much more ambitious. He had spent his life changing the world of entertainment. Now, Walt wanted to alter the way people lived.

He became occupied—then later obsessed—with building a city of the future; a real place where people would sleep, work, and play. No slums. No

155

pollution. No crime. The time wasn't right to start sharing his thoughts, though. A few more pieces had to fall into place first. For the moment, Walt had to keep his ideas to himself and a few close associates.

For all those who had no idea what Walt was planning, his involvement in New York's 1964 World's Fair was a mystery. Why should a man who devoted his life to making durable pieces of entertainment waste his time on a project that would close after a short while? "For the life of me, I couldn't understand why he was interested," said Dick Nunis.

But Walt knew why. "The World's Fair was a chance to experiment with someone else's money," explained Marty Sklar, a Disney writer who had started working for Walt in the early days of Disneyland.

He agreed to create four major attractions: the Carousel of Progress, for General Electric; It's a Small World, for Pepsi Cola; the Magic Skyway, for Ford Motors; and Great Moments with Mr. Lincoln, for the state of Illinois.

Walt revelled in the ability to develop new ideas like Audio-Animatronics: robotlike simulations of real creatures with cogs, pullies, and gears moving their arms, legs, and mouths. The Jungle Cruise animals and the birds in Disneyland's Enchanted Tiki Room had been a start, but it was at the New York World's Fair that Walt's animated three-dimensional figures reached a whole new level of achievement with Abraham Lincoln.

Honest Abe had 48 different body actions and 15 facial movements. Alarmingly, when he was first shipped to New York, the sixteenth president of the United States shook and trembled and weaved and occasionally smashed chairs as he sat down. "Every time an elevator ran by and we had a drop in current, it was exactly like an epileptic fit," said John Hench. "My God, he was a terrifying guy."

After a week's delay to calm Mr. Lincoln down, the show was so convincing that some spectators thought they remembered Mr. Lincoln walking to the end of the stage and shaking hands with people in the audience.

By the time the fair ended, nearly fifty million people had seen one of Walt's four attractions. The tough East-Coast audience generally agreed that Walt's exhibits were among the best in the fair. He brought It's a Small World, Mr. Lincoln, and the Carousel of Progress back to Disneyland. Walt had been able to experiment cheaply with a whole range of ideas including new ways to control crowds and move audiences. Perhaps most important, he had figured

© Walt Disney Enterprises

*Walt clowns around with a dinosaur from the Ford exhibit at the 1964 World's Fair.*

out how to work with large American companies to bring their ideas and dreams directly to the public.

In 1964, the Disney company started to buy thousands of acres of cypress-covered swampland just southwest of Orlando, Florida.

Walt's representatives in Florida kept the name of the buyer a deep dark secret. Had anyone known Walt's plans, the waterlogged, alligator-infested bogs would have become as expensive as downtown Miami. When Walt visited, he went by a fake name, Walter E. Davis. Rumors flew that Ford Motors or McDonnell Douglas were the buyers.

Word began to leak out that Disney was buying the land in the fall of 1965. Prices skyrocketed from less than $200 an acre to around $1,000 an acre. But Walt was nearly finished by then. For $5 million he had purchased about 43 square miles of Florida—twice the size of Manhattan island, nearly 150 times bigger than Disneyland.

On November 15, Walt, Roy, and Florida's governor, Haydon Burns, held a press conference. "Will it be Disneyland?" the governor asked Walt.

Walt wasn't ready to tell anyone what he had in mind. He conceded that the new place might just be called Disney World, but he wouldn't commit to that. He hemmed and hawed about details. Then one of the journalists asked a question that must have startled Walt: "Is it possible that it will be what we think of as a city of tomorrow . . . something we expect to live in thirty, forty years from now?"

At first, Walt danced around the question, but a few minutes later he revealed a bit of what he had on his mind. "I would like to be part of building . . . a city of tomorrow, as you might say . . . facilities for the community . . . community entertainments. . . . I'd love to be part of building up a school of tomorrow. . . ."

Just as Walt was beginning to get rolling, a reporter asked a question that got him off the point. Little more was said of importance except that Walt intended to rely on corporate support for whatever he was doing.

Back at WED, a special planning room was set up for the city Walt decided to call EPCOT, for the Experimental Prototype Community of Tomorrow. Only three men had the keys: Marvin Davis, a talented architect and designer who had married Walt's niece, Marjorie; Joe Potter, a retired Air Force general who had worked with Walt on the World's Fair; and Walt.

Walt sketched designs for EPCOT constantly; on pads, sketching paper, even paper napkins. Twenty-thousand people would rent homes in EPCOT. Everyone would work. "One of our requirements is that the people who live in EPCOT must help keep it alive," Walt said.

"He'd talk for hours about the houses and how the kids would go to school," said Marvin Davis. "He'd even talk for hours about the garbage disposal. He was really engrossed in it. And of course, we became engrossed, too."

Large companies would have the opportunity to try out their latest inventions. In exchange for acting as guinea pigs, residents of EPCOT could experience the newest and most exciting creations before anyone else. Walt and his small band toured the usually classified research departments of major corporations like General Motors, General Electric, and Xerox.

Public transportation preoccupied him. He believed it could be clean, safe, fast, quiet, and energy efficient. "I'm not against the automobile," he had said at the first press conference, "but I just feel that the automobile has moved into communities too much."

Above all, Walt's plans for EPCOT demonstrated his faith in the basic goodness of mankind. He believed that if you gave people a good place to live and the proper information and choices to make it better, they would do so.

A comment Walt had once made about Disneyland was very appropriate to his plans for EPCOT. "You don't build it for yourself," he had said. "You know what the people want and you build it for them."

# Looking to the Future

"*I'm not Walt Disney anymore.*"
—WALT DISNEY

© Walt Disney Enterprises

*The reinvention of transportation for EPCOT Center*

In the early 1950s, Walt had seemed confident that life stretched before him like an endless merry-go-round ride with countless brass rings to be captured and cherished. "Longevity seems to run with the Disneys on both sides of the family," Walt had written when his Uncle Robert turned 85 in April, 1951. "My heart and other vital organs, along with the history of my ancestry, all indicate that I am going to live a long life," he wrote in another letter a month later.

But by the mid-1960s, Walt began to have indications that the merry-go-round might be slowing down a bit. Daily he went to the studio nurse, Hazel George, for massages on his aching back. She became one of his closest friends. He was victim to frequent colds and sinus attacks. He grew winded quickly; when he tried to dance a bit of "Knees up, Mother Brown," which inspired one of the dances in *Mary Poppins*, he lasted only a few minutes. His rasping cigarette cough was constant.

His face became pasty and pale. Television cameramen tried to disguise obvious aging by blurring his image on-screen, but Walt objected, "I feel it is definitely wrong to photograph me with gauze filters. . . . If I cannot stand being too close to the camera, then have them move back somewhat, but no more filters."

160

In Walt's childhood, his sister, Ruth, was always impressed at "how very gritty Walt was"—how you'd never know from him that he was hurt. True to form, he rarely complained now. In fact, he really didn't like to dwell on sickness or death—his own or anyone else's. He never went near Forest Lawn Memorial Park, where his parents were buried. He stayed away from funerals. Even when his brother, Herbert, died in 1961, he didn't go to the services. "Dad was scheduled to go to an air-force base that afternoon," recalled Diane, "and Ron went with him. I remember standing by the grave and I saw a plane overhead and I've always thought it was Dad."

There was certainly no talk of slowing down at the studio or WED. "I can't retire because these guys expect me to be here," he said.

While nobody will ever know whether Walt worried that his productive years might be coming to an end, he began to put his financial affairs in order. "When I'm up in heaven playing the harp, I really couldn't put my heart into it if I thought I had left things in a mess down here," Walt wrote to Roy in May, 1963.

Photo credit: Rush Johnson

*While visiting Marceline, Walt considered building an amusement site in his old hometown.*

161

Whatever he was thinking, his activity was more feverish than ever. He surrounded himself with books and articles about city planning for EPCOT. His television show and the studio called for constant attention. At every opportunity he played with his growing brood of grandchildren; Jennifer arrived in May, 1960, and in November, 1961, Walter Elias Disney Miller was born and Walt finally had his namesake. Two years later, Diane had her sixth child, Ronald, and by the beginning of 1966, Sharon had given birth to a daughter, Victoria. Walt was the first visitor at the hospital. "Of course, he knew everything about children," Sharon laughed. "He said, 'She's going to have great eyes, I can tell she has great eyes.' "

Walt and Lilly travelled extensively—often with Sharon and her husband, Bob, who had joined the staff of WED.

They visited England, and yielded to Walt's desire to search for Disney ancestors. He went to the 1964 Republican Convention in San Francisco.

There were other trips and other activities. In addition to EPCOT, Walt was starting more new ventures than most people could conceive in a lifetime:

He leased land in central California to create a $35 million skiing playground called Mineral King. He talked to people in his hometown about purchasing land there—including his family's old farm—to create "Walt Disney's Boyhood Home," a nonprofit tourist sight that would help Marceline's economy.

He personally supervised the design of New Orleans Square in Disneyland.

He oversaw the redesign of many of the old Disneyland attractions, including the Jungle Cruise, which was altered to replace realism with humor.

Particularly close to his heart was his idea for a new kind of university education for creative people, to be called CalArts. The Chouinard Art Institute, which had trained Disney artists for so long, merged with the Los Angeles Conservatory of Music in 1962. For a number of years, Walt had been contributing to the financially shaky art institute, as well as personally assisting the founder, Mrs. Nelbert Chouinard. With the merger, Walt and Roy saw an opportunity to start a university that could educate students in all facets of the arts—dance, music, drama, painting, film. Students wouldn't be pigeonholed in any one form. They would learn to appreciate all forms of art. "Those who can pay will pay," Walt told the press, "those who can't will get scholarships. . . . We want people with talent."

Walt's mind overflowed with ideas for making his school different from any that went before it. Closed-circuit televisions would connect dance floors with

*Originally, the Jungle Cruise attraction was meant to be as realistic as possible. In its redesign, humorous touches were added, as evidenced in this planning sketch showing frightened natives trapped in a tree.*

© Walt Disney Enterprises

painting rooms, for instance. That way, artists could draw ballerinas at work.

Walt even considered teaching there himself. "I'd like to give a class, too," he told Marc Davis.

Davis looked at him quizzically.

Walt laughed. "Not in drawing. . . . I'm a pretty good story man, you know."

Building . . . building. Walt was always building toward something new or better. He was now often compared with Thomas Edison and Henry Ford, men who had given America its unique shape and form. Some called him an egomaniac; they thought that he promoted his name and reputation for its own sake. But that wasn't the way Walt thought.

One afternoon in 1965, Marty Sklar, one of Walt's writers, approached him with a plan for the corporate annual report. He had written biographies of a number of people who worked for Walt—to demonstrate that the Disney organization was made up of more than just one man.

"I don't want to do this," Walt said. "I'll tell you why," he went on. "Walt Disney is a thing. An image that people have in their minds. And I spent my whole life building it. Walt Disney the person isn't that image, necessarily. I drink and I smoke and there's a whole lot of other things that I do that I don't want to be part of that image.

"I'm not Walt Disney anymore."

# Good-bye

© Walt Disney Enterprises

*"Dad had such faith in his doctors. He thought doctors were magicians."*
—DIANE DISNEY MILLER

On New Year's Day, 1966, Walt was the Grand Marshal of the Tournament of Roses Parade. Surrounded by beautiful girls and fabulous floral floats, he smiled and waved at the crowds.

He would not live to see New Year's Day, 1967.

For the most part, the year was much like any other. Mornings, Walt spent at the studio, which was then working on *The Happiest Millionaire* and an animated feature, *The Jungle Book*. Many afternoons he was at WED, where he planned EPCOT and Disney World.

Roy talked about wanting to retire. He was 72 years old and weary. Walt talked him out of it. He needed his older brother for the grand projects that awaited.

His mind was much on his hometown. In late May, Walt donated a ride from Disneyland—the Midget Autopia—to Marceline, Missouri. It was the only Disneyland ride ever moved elsewhere.

Walt and Lilly celebrated their 41st anniversary in June with Diane and

Ron, Sharon and Bob, and seven grandchildren aboard a huge yacht, which cruised the islands near Vancouver, Canada.

Diane recalled Walt as unusually calm on the trip. He didn't complain about the pain he was obviously feeling. He admitted to being easily "pooped." He limped as the stabbing pangs in his back coursed down his left leg. Still, he was unbothered by the hectic excitement of seven grandchildren. "For peace and quiet he'd go to the top deck and sit there in the wind," Diane said. "He had on a windbreaker and he'd read his books about city planning."

Shortly after they got back, Walt went to the UCLA Medical Center for tests. They found that he needed an operation to relieve the pain in his neck and back. But that could wait until the winter.

Work proceeded apace. At a press conference, Walt was asked what his favorite attraction was at Disneyland. He launched into a long description of a ride that would include pirate ships and treasure. The journalists didn't know what he was talking about. It was Pirates of the Caribbean, which wouldn't be finished for another few years. Walt's favorite ride always was the next one.

Plans for EPCOT continued. Walt decided to make a twenty-minute film about the idea to help other people understand what he was driving at. He pushed the writers to move quickly so that he could have the film done before he checked into the hospital.

In late October, he and Lilly went with Sharon and Bob to Williamsburg, Virginia. The purpose of the trip was a speech to the American Forestry Service. But Walt enjoyed being a tour guide for Sharon and Bob who had never been to the reconstructed town before. They stayed in one of the reproduced colonial houses there.

"It was over Halloween and the leaves were all dropping deep in the streets," recalled Sharon. "It was raining on Halloween night and one little boy came to the door for trick or treat. We hadn't thought of it. I remember Daddy going from room to room trying to find anything. And he finally found something upstairs for this little boy. It was a pack of gum. It had really bothered him to have nothing for him."

By the time Walt returned from Williamsburg he was in constant pain. He went back to his doctors. On Wednesday, November 2, they took X rays and found that he had cancer. The cigarettes he had smoked for over 40 years had caused a walnut-sized lump in his left lung.

Lilly was concerned, but she didn't understand—or want to understand—

how serious the news was. She told Diane and Sharon. Walt's cheery attitude made them optimistic that everything would return to normal after an operation the following Monday.

When Roy referred to the disease as a "carcinoma," the Latin term for it, his daughter-in-law, Patty, corrected him. "Grandpa," she said innocently, "that's cancer." Roy exploded, and Patty ran from the room in tears. In the 1960s, many people avoided using the word cancer. It was such a terrifying disease that its very name frightened people. They referred to the "Big C," or "It," as in "He has It."

Walt continued to go in to the studio for the next few days. Peter Ellenshaw saw him in the hall. "You look like you're really hurting," said the artist, who had come to depend on Walt for inspiration and encouragement.

"Well, it's my back injury. You know, from playing polo I got a back injury. I'm going to have an operation."

Ellenshaw's face showed concern and fear.

Walt read the artist's thoughts. "I'm not going over there to die," he said. "There's no problem." He walked away.

And Ellenshaw thought, "My God, my great man is going to die."

On Monday, November 7, Walt went in for the operation. Lilly and her two daughters waited anxiously in his hospital room. The surgeon entered, unsmiling. Time stopped for the three women as the doctor bluntly told them that he had removed Walt's left lung. The cancer had spread, he said, and Walt had between six months and two years to live.

Walt spent two more weeks in the hospital, right across the street from the studio. The day he got out, November 21, he called his secretary and asked to be picked up and brought to the studio.

Everyone was shocked at how thin and weak he looked. He held conferences and talked about plans for a movie called *The Horse in the Gray Flannel Suit*. Over lunch in the company cafeteria, he told some of his closest associates that they had taken out his left lung. "He said that they were confident that they had gotten all the cancer out, and that he was confident, too, and that it was just a question of resting up," said John Hench.

After lunch, he headed for WED—just as he'd done almost every day for years. The secretaries in the office tried to wait on him, but he wasn't going to accept any sick man treatment. "I'm all right," he told them. "I can do it."

He stopped by Marc Davis's office. Davis, another of the nine old men, had worked closely with Walt since the mid-1930s on virtually every important project from *Bambi* to Disneyland to the early plans for EPCOT. A gifted artist, he was then working on sketches of preposterous-looking bears for Mineral King. "He sat down in the chair," said Davis, "and I had the drawings up of the bear band. They were a funny bunch and Walt laughed. He looked like hell."

"I said, 'They sure knocked the weight off of you.' He looked at me with big sad eyes and God, I could have bitten my tongue off."

Walt spent a little while more with Davis and some of the other WED employees. Then, he decided he had to get going. He left Davis at his office. "I stayed at the door," Davis recalled, "and watched him walk down the hall. He was, I guess, about 50 feet away. He turned and said, 'Good-bye Marc.'

"He never said good-bye. It was always 'see ya later.'"

Walt went back to the studio two more times. He stopped by the set where they were shooting *Blackbeard's Ghost* with Peter Ustinov. "I have lung cancer," he told the actor, "but I'm going to lick it."

Many studio employees already knew. Rumors had flown back and forth between the doctors and nurses on one side of Buena Vista Street and studio employees on the other. Behind closed doors, teary-eyed employees wondered aloud, "What will we do now? Who can take over for such a man?"

Walt spent most of the next couple of weeks at home with Lilly. He visited his children and grandchildren. When Diane brought him a drink and a little plate, he mistook it for an ashtray and looked at her like she had lost her mind. "I don't smoke, kid," he told her. Then a long pause. "But they're still not sure that smoking causes lung cancer."

He made plans for cutting back on his activities. "I'm not going to worry about motion pictures any more," he told Ron. "I'm going to concentrate on the parks and building EPCOT." He spent one night at the family's house in Palm Springs, but came home the next day.

On November 30, Walt returned to the hospital. His condition worsened quickly, and he was often in a drug-induced fog. He refused to see anyone but his immediate family.

Roy was ever-present by his bedside, often talking about business. *The Happiest Millionaire* was nearly done. Walt thought it was going to be a hit. When Walt slept, Roy sat silently by, lost in thought. When the girls visited, Walt greeted them with a wave of the hand and a "Hiya, kid," that steadily weakened as the days dragged on. One time when Ron stopped by he introduced his son-in-law to a nurse.

"This is my son," Walt said.

"You mean your son-in-law," the nurse corrected.

"No, I mean my son."

Peter Ellenshaw painted him a picture of a smoke tree, but Walt wouldn't allow him to deliver it in person. Walt had it hung in the room, and pointed it out to his nurses. "See that? One of my boys painted that for me."

In the hours he spent alone, Walt stared at the ceiling above his bed. He used the grid formed by its foot-square tiles to plan out EPCOT.

At 9:35 on the morning of December 15, Walt Disney died.

"I don't think he believed it would ever happen," Ward Kimball said. "I don't think he accepted it, knowing Walt. Not until he closed his eyes for the last time was he ever convinced."

# Closing Up the Books

*"When he died, it was really extraordinary how it affected us. I would wake up crying at night."*
—PETER ELLENSHAW
*Artist*

© Walt Disney Enterprises

"I remember standing in the hospital hallway right after Walt died," said Roy's daughter-in-law, Patty Disney, "and my father-in-law was consumed with grief. I'd never seen him cry before that. I put my arm around him and he walked away. He wanted to be alone."

"I heard the report on the news," said Ruth. "It was said so casually, then they went right on to the next item."

"I really didn't know he was going to go," said Lilly. "Neither did he. We had a trip planned for him to recover."

The news of Walt's illness had been kept secret from the press. Now, the world mourned. Newspapers, television, magazines all poured out stories of love and grief for a man who had given so much.

Television commentator Eric Severeid's eulogy was particularly memorable. "He was an original," said Severeid on the CBS Evening News. "Not just an American original, but an original, period. He was a happy accident; one of the happiest this century has experienced; and judging by the way it's been behaving in spite of all Disney tried to tell it about laughter, love, children,

170

puppies, and sunrises, the century hardly deserved him. . . . People are saying we'll never see his like again."

Contrary to rumor, Walt was cremated—not frozen and put away to be thawed at some later date. The funeral itself was as Walt had wanted it, a very small, private affair. "I don't want anyone to go through that for me," he had said, and his family respected his wishes. Even Ruth wasn't there. "They said the news media would follow me," she remembered.

When Walt's secretary cleaned out his office, she found surprises. She called Sharon. "I've found boxes and boxes of things of Walt's," she said. "I think you might want them."

There were postcards and letters and notes from his daughters, Diane's bronzed baby shoes, and all sorts of other mementos of his family. "All those years and none of us knew he kept those things," said Sharon.

In the days following Walt's death an enormous question lingered: Would Disney World be canceled? The project had just been getting off the ground. Now, with its guiding spirit gone, it could be just as easily forgotten.

© Walt Disney Enterprises

*Roy at the opening of Walt Disney World. At Roy's insistence, the park's name was changed from "Disney World," "so people will always known that it was Walt's dream."*

171

"When he died, we all said, 'There goes Disney World,' " recalled Marvin Davis. "Then, Roy called a meeting in the main studio projection room. And all the main people who were involved in Disney World were there. I've never heard a more profoundly brave, gutsy speech in my life. He had just buried his brother, and he was giving us all a pep talk.

"He said, 'Walt would want us to face this opportunity and by God, we're going to do it!'

"When we walked out of there, everybody shook hands and said, 'Well, we're going to finish it.' "

In October, 1971, the first part of the Florida complex opened. Only it wasn't just called Disney World. Roy insisted that the new park be called Walt Disney World "so people will always know that it was Walt's dream."

After the opening, Roy had long phone conversations with his older brother, Ray, and his sister, Ruth. "It was like he was closing up his books," recalled Patty Disney.

Two months after Walt Disney World opened, on December 21, Roy died of a cerebral hemorrhage. He had been watching out for Walt since they were boys. Now, he had held onto life just long enough to take care of his brother's biggest dream.

# The Dream Goes On

*"Gee, this is an exciting age. The next fifty years are going to be just terrific."*
—WALT DISNEY

*From*
The Little Mermaid

Several years ago, Lorraine Santoli, then supervisor of publicity for Disneyland, talked about Walt Disney. "His spirit is really alive and all of us who work here feel that," she said of the man she had never met. "You have a sense that Walt might be peeking around the corner."

Walt has been gone for over thirty years now, yet his impact on the world of entertainment, on his close friends and colleagues, and of course, on his family is still felt.

Bill Cottrell, Walt's brother-in-law, confidant, and top executive, retired from the Disney organization in 1981 after nearly fifty-three years with the company. He passed away in 1996. Until the end of his life, he continued to speak of Walt as though he were still alive, as in, "Walt is a great man to travel with."

Cottrell isn't the only one who continued to preserve Walt's memory in a passionate way. "When I find myself referring to Walt, it's not in the past tense," recalls Tom Nabbe, who played Tom Sawyer at Disneyland when he was a teenager.

"Walt had such a wonderful reputation around the world—and he still does," says Dick Nunis, Chairman of Walt Disney Attractions. "People think he's still alive."

When Walt died, he left more than his family and company and characters. He left many dreams. But how could they be made reality? No one ever knew much about Walt's plans for the future when he was alive. Since he was always several steps ahead of everyone else, it was virtually impossible to guess what his next step would have been. Yet in the years following his death, one question pervaded the halls and offices of the studio: "What would Walt have done?"

Of all Walt's dreams, EPCOT was the biggest question mark. It would have been a giant step forward for the company—from creating entertainment for millions of people to actually creating a place for them to live. Walt had had architectural plans drawn up as a starting point for fulfilling this vision. He had steeped himself in research about city planning. He had talked incessantly about sanitation, transportation, and all the other elements that EPCOT would require.

But, without his vision, the idea of moving forward with Walt's EPCOT seemed impossible to those who remained behind, including his brother Roy.

Instead, EPCOT became closer to a world's fair that combines education and entertainment. In World Showcase, a variety of countries such as France, England, Canada, Italy, Germany, Japan, and China have a chance to show their customs, foods, crafts, horticulture, even architecture and art to visitors. In Future World, pavilions that focus on the land, the seas, health, transportation, energy, and the imagination give sponsoring companies the chance to showcase new products while visitors float, ride, or walk amidst elaborate Audio-Animatronics scenes, demonstrations of futuristic farming, and magnificent aquariums.

Some of Walt's dreams died. Mineral King was derailed by environmental groups that objected to the use of the land for a tourist attraction. Walt Disney's Boyhood Home also never materialized, although Marceline began in 1998 to honor Walt's hundredth birthday. The hometown party will include a series of events showcasing influences on Walt's life from dance, music, art, and theater—culminating in 2001 with a grand celebration.

Other of his works thrived, CalArts, the university that Walt helped found, now has about one thousand students and five schools that cover art, dance, music, video, and theater.

Disneyland, meanwhile, has continued to prosper. New attractions have been added; others have been dropped. In fact, Walt's early delight that "even the trees will keep growing" in Disneyland has become something of an irony. As it turned out, the trees on Main Street have grown so well that they can make it difficult to see the castle from various vantage points.

In films, the company floundered during the 1970s, then began to revive with the creation of Touchstone, and the release of its first picture, *Splash*, in 1984. The movie division was started by son-in-law Ron Miller, who was Chief Executive Officer in the early 1980s. By introducing a new label, the company could now take on more sophisticated film projects that went beyond standard Disney fare. Miller also started the Disney Channel.

A corporate reorganization in 1984 put the leadership of the company in the hands of Michael Eisner, formerly president of Paramount Pictures. In the years that followed, successful movies such as *Angels in the Outfield* and *George of the Jungle* were released. The company renewed its commitment to animation with a series of successful animated features including *The Little Mermaid, Beauty and the Beast,* and most recently *Mulan*. It even expanded into Broadway with *Beauty and the Beast* and a Tony Award–winning musical based on the animated film *The Lion King.*

Ironically, about forty years after Walt needed ABC's support to raise the money for Disneyland, the Disney Company purchased the TV network outright.

Re-releases of Walt's films—both in theaters and on videotape—have proved that his dedication to quality was worthwhile. Long before anyone knew the value of "repeat" business, Walt urged his artists, directors, and writers to shy away from current affairs, trendy gags, or anything that would limit the appeal of his productions to one country or one generation. The company will reap the benefits for decades to come.

Although Michael Eisner never met Walt, he grew up watching the man on television and yearning to see Disneyland. His background, he says, is about as different from Walt's as anyone's can be. But he shares the founder's respect for quality. Does he think about Walt much? "I use him," he said. "If someone wants to make a shortcut or save a little money on this or the other thing, I remind everybody of what our mission is here."

Meanwhile, Walt continues to be a powerful and loving presence to the family members he left behind. Sadly, his daughter Sharon died in 1993. She had lost her first husband to cancer shortly after Walt's death, and later remarried and had twins, Brad and Michelle.

All Walt's brothers and his sister have passed away as well, Raymond in 1989 and Ruth in 1995.

In 1998, Lilly died. She passed away peacefully in the home she and Walt built in 1950. Though the soda fountain and train tracks had been removed, much of the miniature furniture Walt designed was still proudly displayed in an alcove just inside the entranceway. Several years before her death, she made two donations for the creation of Walt Disney Hall, a concert hall to be located in Los Angeles: one for $50 million another for $25 million.

Diane and Ron Miller had a seventh child, a son named Patrick, in 1967. Today, they are happily involved in a variety of projects and run Silverado Vineyards, a Northern California winery. The preservation of Walt's memory in a fair and accurate manner has become a project of great importance to Diane and her family. Toward that end, they were the guiding force behind the creation of a multimedia interactive biography of Walt, released in the fall of 1998.

For the same reason, Diane has donated Walt's red barn—where he used to work on his train—to Griffith Park in Los Angeles, where it can be enjoyed by countless children and adults.

Meanwhile, Walt's ten grandchildren continue to move forward in a variety of endeavors. The older ones, who were born early enough to have clear memories of Walt, treasure those recollections.

"The fact that you walked in the door made him happy," recalls Jennifer.

"He took such pleasure in us," says Tamara. "He just seemed to enjoy us interacting in front of him, and never told us to be quiet."

"About ten years ago I started wondering how in the world did he do everything he did and spend all that time with us?" says Joanna. "I miss him so much right now."

She is not alone.

# Index

# Index

# Index

ACKNOWLEDGMENTS

Throughout our reporting for this book, we were gratified by the kindness of almost everyone we approached. A complete list of all those who worked with us would go on for a dozen pages or more, but here we would like to thank some of those who were particularly generous with their time, memories, thoughts, and comments.

Walt Disney's family was instrumental in a variety of ways, including submitting to repeated interviews, putting us in touch with others who knew Walt well, and providing encouragement all along the way. We want to especially thank Walt's children, Diane Disney Miller, her husband Ron Miller, and Sharon Disney Lund. Without them we would not have been able to complete this book. In addition, we were thrilled to have the opportunity to talk with Walt's widow, Lillian Disney, his sister, Ruth Disney Beecher, Roy's son, Roy E. Disney, and his daughter-in-law, Patty Disney, Walt's brother-in-law and co-worker Bill Cottrell, and Walt's nephews and nieces, Marjorie Davis, Marvin Davis, Dorothy Puder, and Glen Puder.

We also want to take special note of the constant support of Cheryl Davis and Linda Berg of the Disney public relations department and of Bo Boyd, president of Disney Consumer Products.

In addition to scores of personal interviews, we were privileged to spend many weeks working in the Disney archives. They are a biographer's dream. In that connection, we owe an enormous debt to the head archivist, David Smith, and his able co-workers, Paula Sigman and Rose Motzko.

Other current and past employees and associates of the Disney company who were particularly helpful include Sherry Alberoni, Sharon Baird, Bobby Burgess, Tommy Cole, Tim Considine, Myriam Estany, Marc and Alice Davis, Ron Dominguez, Michael Eisner, Peter Ellenshaw, Annette Funicello, Harper Goff, John Hench, David Herbst, Ollie Johnston, Ward Kimball, Arlene Ludwig, Bob Moore, Hayley Mills, Fred MacMurray, Wayne Morris, Tom Nabbe, Erwin Okun, Richard Nunis, Fess Parker, Elizabeth Richman, Charles Ridgeway, Herb Ryman (and his sister, Lucille Carroll), Lorraine Santoli, Marty Sklar, Frank Thomas, and Dick Van Dyke.

Our trips to Kansas City and Marceline were met with enormous Midwestern hospitality. Among those who aided us in our efforts to reassemble Walt's youth in Missouri were Marguerite Beverforden, Rosemary Beymer, William Brown, Mr. and Mrs. Dick Dotteridge, Clem Flickinger, Rush Johnson, Kay Malins, Meyer Minda, Helen Mundy, Mr. and Mrs. Willam Mundy, Mr. and Mrs. Lawrence Stalling, Mary Maxine Vanderpool, and the principal and staff of the D.A. Holmes School (formerly the Benton School).

Of course, we used much existing material, but we must single out a few sources for special mention: a series of interviews recorded with Walt Disney by Diane Miller and journalist Pete Martin in the late fifties; Bob Thomas's authoritative book, *Walt Disney: An American Original*; and Leonard Maltin's *Of Mice and Magic* and the *The Disney Films*.

Thanks must also go to our agent, Stuart Krichevsky, and our editors at Viking, Nancy Paulsen and Stephanie Hutter, who conspired to protect us from the nightmares of the book publishing world as much as possible.

Finally, we would be remiss not to mention the name of our nephew, and Disney-o-phile, Andrew Barrett-Weiss. When he was 14, we went in search of a biography of Walt Disney to buy him. None existed that fit the bill. That was the beginning of the road that led to this book.